No Quick Fix

No Quick Fix

A church's mission to the London drugs scene

Eric Blakebrough

Marshall Pickering

Marshall Morgan and Scott
Marshall Pickering
3 Beggarwood Lane, Basingstoke, Hants RG23 7LP, UK

Copyright © 1986 by Eric Blakebrough

First published in 1986 by Marshall Morgan and Scott Publications Ltd
Part of the Marshall Pickering Holdings Group
A subsidiary of the Zondervan Corporation

 Reprinted : Impression number
87 88 89 90 : 10 9 8 7 6 5 4 3 2

British Library CIP Data

Blakebrough, Eric
 No quick fix: a church's mission to the London drug scene.
 1. Church work with narcotic addicts—England—London
 I. Title
 259   BV4470

 ISBN 0 551 01323 0

Text set in Plantin by Brian Robinson, North Marston, Bucks
Printed in Great Britain by Hazell Watson & Viney Ltd, Member of
the BPCC Group, Aylesbury, Bucks.

To Mary, Justin, Adele and Martin

Contents

Preface

This is a true story about real people. The Kaleidoscope Club is very much still in existence at 40–46 Cromwell Road, Kingston-upon-Thames, Surrey. You can visit the place and have lunch there. The club is still open all night from 10 p.m. on Fridays. The John Bunyan Church is 103 years old. It has changed radically in those years and is still changing.

The names of many people in the book have been changed where this has been appropriate to protect the confidentiality of their relationship with Kaleidoscope. Real names are used for church members and Kaleidoscope staff. Some lapses in objectivity are inevitable, but I have tried to give a fair and honest account of the last 17 years.

They have been unbelievable years, peopled by some of the strangest, as well as some of the most visionary individuals anyone could wish to meet. There has been much excitement, occasional terror, but no end to the challenge.

Eric Blakebrough.
August, 1985.

Acknowledgments

It would be impossible to thank individually all the members of John Bunyan Baptist Church, the staff of Kaleidoscope, and others in the Royal Borough of Kingston-upon-Thames who, by their support over many years, made this story possible. But there are some I must mention by name.

First, Ian Hargreaves, who turned my manuscript into good prose. I have attempted few enterprises during the years covered by this book without first consulting Ian and his wife Liz. My debt to them is enormous.

My thanks are also due to a series of excellent Assistant Ministers, David Langridge, Julie Hopkins, Andrew Mawson and most recently my daughter, Adele Blakebrough-Fairbairn.

Everyone involved in Kaleidoscope owes much to George Short, who has served us as administrator for more than seven years. Most of all, and most deeply, Mary, my wife, and I are grateful to Alan and Uschi Roberts. Their love and hard work have turned dreams and visions into realities.

1: Deaths And Entrances

'POLICE RAID CLUB AFTER FIVE FOUND DEAD.'

That front page headline, in the *Kingston Borough News*, January 25, 1974, was the first thing most residents of the Royal Borough of Kingston heard about the John Bunyan Baptist Church's Kaleidoscope Club.

Like a lot of newspaper headlines, it was misleading, but inviting. Kingston, in common with other parts of several big cities, was in the middle of a wave of acute public concern about drug addiction. Derelict buildings around the town had been converted into 'squats', where young people could live cheaply, communally and sometimes dangerously. The numbers of registered drug addicts—then as now the finest tip of a considerably larger iceberg—was growing, but the values of youth culture were ambiguous on the point. The Beatles had broken up and the flower children of San Francisco had departed. But the notion that drugs could expand your mind, subvert competitive, commercial values and foster peace hung on.

The *Borough News* story went on to explain, on the basis of events recounted in the magistrates' court, how police had raided the Kaleidoscope Club in the hope of smashing an evil drugs ring. A number of the club's regulars were in court facing charges of obstructing the police, assault on the police and possession of illegal substances. In recent months, officers explained to the bench, five young people had died in the borough as a result of drug incidents. They

11

had to crack down on such activity, even if it meant invading church premises in the middle of the night. The police were confident, and reasonably so, that their actions had the support of the community at large. People were and still are frightened of the menace of drug addiction, which appears to strike at random into the lives of otherwise healthy, happy and even affluent young people.

I first heard of that headline at 7.30 on Saturday morning, when my telephone rang. The editor of the *Borough News* explained that he had been on holiday and returned to see the latest edition of his newspaper. The headline horrified him. He checked with his legal advisers and they told him bluntly it was almost certainly libellous. He hoped I would take a generous view.

Hardly awake, having been up all the previous night in the club, I only gradually realised the effect that headline would have on people. It was difficult to understand how I had ever become involved in running an all-night club, in being caught up in the drug scene, in being a victim of police raids and now the centre of sensational publicity.

I had become the minister of the John Bunyan Baptist Church in Kingston-upon-Thames four years previously. It seemed almost accidental that I had become the pastor of this church. I had been an industrial chaplain in south London and enjoyed trying to work out the meaning of the Kingdom of God in an industrial setting. I had not thought to return to a pastoral charge because I felt that many pastors became captive to their congregation, only serving the needs of believers.

My predecessor at the church had been seriously ill over a long period of time. I agreed to preach when he was indisposed. When I made that first visit to Kingston, I was surprised to find it was not the sleepy market town in leafy

Surrey I had expected. It is, in fact, a thoroughly urban borough; the centre of population for approximately one sixth of the GLC area. The view from Kingston railway station is of cars, shops, pubs, coffee bars and people. The River Thames and Richmond Park are not within sight.

On one occasion when I stood in for the minister, he came to the pulpit at the end of the service and announced that he had to retire on grounds of ill health. He added: 'My successor is in the pulpit.'

That remark was entirely unconstitutional. I had not indicated any wish to return to a pastorate and the church members had not expressed any wish for me to be their new pastor. Afterwards, the church secretary apologised for the remark. Neither the church members nor I had any idea that we would be drawn together in the near future.

Eventually, however, the church decided to approach me. They had tried to find a new minister elsewhere and failed. My first reaction was negative.

The church, almost one hundred years old, had a declining, aging membership. Once in a residential area, it was now on an island at the centre of a one-way traffic system, the railway and Kingston's rapidly growing shopping centre. Its buildings were rambling and decaying. Although the galleried chapel had a nostalgic magnificence, it was a building for a previous age.

Aged 37 at the time, I realised that my next move would be critical for the whole of my ministry. I had been in the Royal Air Force and then at Bristol Baptist College. That had led to an enjoyable first pastorate at Southend-on-Sea, which was followed by a brief stint with the West Ham Central Mission. I then worked as an industrial chaplain under Bishop John Robinson.

This past experience had convinced me that the church ought to be involved not only in seeking to convert individuals,

13

but also in transforming society. I had also had experience of working in an ecumenical setting and had grown to appreciate the sacramental emphasis in the larger Christian denominations.

It did not seem to me that this was the best possible preparation for my future ministry at Kingston. I was hesitant to consider a call from the church, but agreed nonetheless to meet the deacons to consider how I would envisage the future pattern of a ministry in the church.

I said that, in the centre of a town like Kingston, I could not imagine a traditional pattern of ministry being appropriate. I thought that the church would need to concentrate on serving the needs of its neighbourhood, rather than building up its congregation.

Some days later, the deacons invited me to meet them again. We discussed at length the meaning of the Kingdom of God. Among other things, the Kingdom of God refers to the rule of God in the world. A local church, as an agent of the Kingdom of God, must dream dreams and have visions of God's will being worked out in its neighbourhood. The further task of the church is to take the initiatives aimed at transforming the locality into something nearer God's intention.

Obviously this process will only be completed at the end of time and by the intervention of God, but some tentative steps ought to be taken here and now by those who are seeking to be co-workers with Christ.

That is how I described my vision to the members of the church. They shared my enthusiasm and invited me to lead them in that kind of ministry. Mary, my wife, and I pondered this unexpected invitation. We wondered how our three children would react to a move. In the end we were convinced this was the call of God.

Before it could be decided how the church was to serve its

local community, it was necessary to be clear who the church was aiming to serve. The three or four dozen households in the same block as the church hardly constituted a big enough community.

The biggest concentration of people in the church's neighbourhood is two hundred yards to the west, in the area surrounding Kingston Railway Station. What could be done by the church with the people who gathered there?

Headlines in the local newspaper gave a clue. An outbreak of violence and drug abuse among young people, which was particularly serious on Friday nights, was the main running story of the time.

When these reports were first considered at the church meeting, opinions were divided about what could be done. A group of Christians had attempted evangelistic outreach among this crowd in recent years, but this venture was no longer attracting young people from the streets. A recruitment drive for the Boys' Brigade was thought unlikely to succeed.

Mary and I spent some time drinking coffee in one of the local cafés where numbers of young people used to congregate. We observed the general lethargy of the group and overheard their bored conversation.

Tentatively, we entered two or three of the public houses which served the large number of young people who came into the centre of Kingston for entertainment especially at the weekends. We were nearly deafened by the loud music at the Three Fishes. The music was not the chart material we had become accustomed to in previous youth clubs. These sounds were altogether more powerful, played by groups such as Pink Floyd, Led Zeppelin, Jefferson Airplane and the Rolling Stones, who used at one time to play at a Kingston jazz club.

People were dressed in the style of the hippy movement;

the girls looking almost ethereal in their long Indian cotton skirts and the men wearing their hair long. The crowd had the animation of youth, but many seemed to be in a private dream. Mary and I had no previous experience of drug abuse and we did not recognise the signs of hallucinogenic drugs.

The overflow from the Three Fishes was catered for in the next public house we visited. Then, on the opposite side of the road, was the Kingston Hotel, where we found a huge crowd of Skinheads. Their music, based on the West Indian reggae beat, was entirely different. At the third corner of the crossroads was the South Western public house and here we found a meeting of Hell's Angels. They favoured heavy rock music.

Venturing further afield, we found the Swan public house. The music met us as we approched this crowded rock 'n roll establishment. Teddy Boys with long sideburns and thick, crepe soled shoes danced in the style of the 1950s with girls wearing vast circular skirts.

Apart from the public houses, which catered for different groups of young people, there was little else to meet the recreational needs of the young people who poured into the centre of Kingston, especially on a Friday night.

In the Royal Air Force, I had been an NCO in charge of boy entrants. I knew that discos and other recreational facilities were important for people in the forces. Similarly, at university and other places of education, social life is recognised to be almost as important as academic provision. A young person can only form his personal, political and religious opinions by reference to other people's opinions. It is only from mutual exploration and confrontation that people can develop their own personalities.

These observations, and the conviction that life is meant to be enjoyed, made Mary and I strong advocates of open

16

youth clubs. Our observation was that in Kingston many young people were severely deprived of good social experience.

The public houses catered for this need to some extent, but the loud music and restricted hours resulted in a very limited social life. That is why they complained that there was nothing to do in Kingston. It also explained the drift towards impromptu parties in empty houses which occurred after the public houses closed.

These parties were risky affairs. Those who attended them normally had to lie to their parents, telling them, for example, that they were staying with a friend. The parties, being held in property without legal ownership, meant that no one was responsible and things often got out of hand.

The squats were wide open to alcohol, drug abuse and sexual promiscuity. The fact that sensible people avoided such parties made them more dangerous. They attracted many who had no thought-out morals and some who were so depressed they no longer cared for themselves or others. These weekends in squats were therefore high-risk areas for any young person seeking excitement in a town which offered very few creative alternatives.

Mary and I prepared our report for the monthly church members' meeting, making tentative suggestions for how we might meet the needs of young people in the town centre.

The suggestions were heard most attentively by the membership, which was already committed to trying to serve its local community. There were, however, real anxieties. Members were worried that a concentration upon open youth club work might be detrimental to traditional church activities. The active membership was already down to several families, a dozen or so single people and a mere handful of teenagers. Could we really afford to put all our effort into youth work when the church was so weak?

Some members were properly concerned that the groups of young people we had identified might prove too difficult to accommodate. There was a danger that they would wreck the church buildings. The treasurer appeared to deliver the final blow to the whole idea when he said: 'The fact of the matter is, there's no money available for such a scheme.' He explained that there was hardly enough money at the bank or coming to the church in weekly offerings to pay the minister's stipend. There was absolutely no capital available to make any part of the church premises suitable as a youth club. If any money could be found, it was needed to repair the church roof, to rewire the whole premises and to attend to the faulty plumbing.

It is a testimony to the faith and courage of the members that their deliberations finally took a more positive turn. The basic commitment to serving the local community was reaffirmed. The members suggested that people could make interest-free personal loans for this purpose. There was an immediate response and promises of £400 and voluntary labour were made.

Mary and I had created clubs before—in an air-raid shelter in Southend and in the basement of our house in East London during a spell with the West Ham Central Mission. I looked over the John Bunyan Baptist Church and identified the Isaac Stalberg Hall, named after a Victorian minister of the church, as suitable for conversion.

Just as we were beginning to feel more confident about this enterprise, the church secretary received a letter from the relatives of the late Rev Isaac Stalberg. They protested that the conversion of the hall would have appalled Mr Stalberg. This letter echoed misgivings in the hearts of a few of the church members, especially those who no longer attended. One older member, however, commented that if Isaac Stalberg had been alive today, he would have moved with the times and approved of what we were doing. It was agreed that I should remove the memorial plaque in order to save any offence. Perhaps it was significant that we were making a break with the past.

A lot of work went into creating that first Kaleidoscope. The ceiling was lowered, discotheque equipment installed, coffee bar fitted out. There were black walls, pine fittings and an illuminated kaleidoscope emblem. The name was intended to reflect the objectives of an open youth club—to appeal across the fragmented boundaries of youth culture to attract everyone from hippies, with their long hair and dreams, to no-nonsense skinheads and leather-clad bikers.

It didn't work. The food was good, the coffee was good, the place was good, but the people did not come, or at least not in very large numbers.

One day, a 19-year-old Canadian girl called Jan Johnston walked through the door. With her long, curly brown hair and a gentle smile, Jan's most obvious quality was her warmth. A North American openness combined with a softer, more enigmatic quality to give her a definite magnetism.

Jan's long dress and flowing style clearly identified her with the hippy group. She said she liked the idea of a place where there could be a celebration of youth and a focus for action. 'But in a church youth club? I don't really think so. Good luck anyway.'

Good luck or not, numbers at the club started to increase, although Jan was not among them. When she did return, several months later, she looked thinner. Her eyes had a searching, earnest look and she quickly came to the point.

She was living in some kind of commune with two other people, Dave and Andrea. They only worked when they needed money and spent most of their time studying philosophy and religion and practising meditation. 'We figured we should look at Christianity too. Jesus was an important figure and I was interested in what you said about communion between people,' said Jan. 'Would you spend some time at our place and tell us more about it?'

David and Andrea could both have stepped from pre-Raphaelite paintings. Pale skins, long, well-brushed hair and clear eyes. David wore a brightly coloured waistcoat and sandals. When I arrived, the three sat cross-legged on the floor.

They had prepared a large saucepan of vegetable soup and there was a basket of home-made rolls, cheese and some fruit. There would be no need to break the conversation for many hours. That was the expectation.

Apart from the breaks to go home and sleep, we took part in three solid days of conversation. Endless questions and answers. Moments of excitement as some grain of truth fell clear. On that third day, I took a bread roll, said a blessing, broke the bread and initiated the three young people into the Christian Eucharist. Jan, David and Andrea then began regularly to attend church, which brought its own problems and pressures for change.

The attendance at church of a new group of unconventional young people was not welcomed by all members of the congregation. Newcomers were expected to settled down as quickly as possible and conform to the existing order. These young people were unwilling to settled down and challenged the existing order with great intellectual vigour. When they were shortly joined by four other young graduates from Cambridge, some of the members felt increasingly threatened.

Some members of the church now started to attend other churches. Neighbouring Baptist congregations heard disturbing reports about Bunyan. It was said that the minister was only interested in drug addicts and pregnant girls.

Meanwhile, Jan's influence was brought directly to bear on the club. She felt the disco-style atmosphere, although fun, was not one in which young people could really explore ideas and experiences. As she saw it, life should be experienced as a kind of festival. It was partly a matter of taste, but also something deeper. Instead of Top of the Pops dance music, Jan wanted to introduce subtler, more curious musicians, like the Incredible String Band, whose folk-based tunes became for a short time anthems of the culture.

'May the long time sun shine upon you
All love surround you
And the pure light within you
Guide you all the way on.'

The Saturday evening disco continued, but on Friday nights, the new-style Kaleidoscope was open from 10 pm until 6 am the next morning. Decor switched from disco chic to pale blue walls, Piet Mondrian murals and the main piece of furniture was a large, low platform covered in an Oriental rug. This idea was imported by Richard Fitzsimmons, a young, deeply private man who had fled from three uncomfortable years at Cambridge University to try to discover some new purpose. He had seen a similar platform in an 'alternative' club in Amsterdam.

It was a period of great creativity and dashing reflection. Sunday evenings found groups of church members and the new Kaleidoscope influx discussing moral values, politics, history and the Spirit. There was anger, hilarity, bitterness, change and eccentricity. Richard buried his watch in the church garden, declaring that time was the enemy of meaning.

But behind the pure light, there was also darkness. Use of

drugs such as cannabis was promoted by many young people as a source of relaxation without the aggression all too often triggered by the more accepted social drug of alcohol. Powerful hallucinogens like LSD were available and some said allowed users to penetrate new mysteries. Others gained entry only into prolonged nightmares and mental hospitals.

The club was now packed all night, every Friday night, with a group of people for whom these judgments and experiences were a normal part of the social scenery. The effect was sometimes bright, even electric. But some of the kids, very young, looked terrible, especially those whose chief form of escape was to crush up barbiturate sleeping pills ('barbs') and inject them into their veins. They no longer walked properly, but simply leaned forward and let their legs keep them from falling. Often they did fall, sometimes in the road and in front of moving cars. The public had no idea of what happened on the streets at night.

On most club nights in those days some people in the club could be seen to be under the influence of LSD. In most cases, this just made them a little distant—'spaced out' was the phrase used—but in other cases the effect was dramatic. One youth was convinced he saw me in the men's toilet cutting people into pieces and flushing them down the lavatory. He was in a total state of panic, especially whenever I approached, and he went frantically around the club warning people to escape while they could.

On another occasion, a girl was hallucinating and in a state of terror. When club closed at 6 am friends took her home. She became hysterical and since her parents could think of nothing else to do, they put her in their car and drove her to my house. When they arrived, the girl was screaming at the top of her voice, to the dismay of the entire street, that she would not be dragged 'into the vicar's house.'

Treatment in such cases was like the action of a mother comforting a young child in a nightmare. Quiet music, dim lights, reassuring words, were all part of the treatment. The only problem was to keep this up, possibly for as long as four hours, until the effect of the drug wore off.

Kaleidoscope, in a way, became part of the street. It saw the celebration and the delight, but it also saw the self-destruction. One Saturday morning, as volunteer staff were sweeping the club after breakfast, they found a figure still slumped in a corner of the club.

She said her name was Theresa and that she had nowhere to go. She was heavy with drugs, but not incapacitated. After some conversation, I gathered the impression that she had lived in children's homes, but Theresa agreed to be driven to her parents' home—a council house about five miles away.

At that early hour, Theresa's mother seemed not so much shocked to see her daughter, as to be lifting an eyelid from a permanent state of shell-shock in the relationship. She made tea and said little. Her husband came down, drank tea and ate and also said little. Theresa curled up in a ball on the floor in a corner of the room like an animal attempting to hibernate.

I never really found out Theresa's story. Her father had a successful motorbike business. They were a Catholic family. She had gone to a convent school in well-to-do Wimbledon. But she was already, at the age of 16, beyond the reach of her parents. Her life was in fact built around an obsession with obtaining drugs, legally or illegally. She had been thrown out of school for a drug offence. Her best friend Laura had died from an overdose.

There was no difficulty persuading the parents that their daughter should go to live with Jan, who by now had taken possession of the crumbling church caretaker's house, alongside the Kaleidoscope Club, with the objective of creating a commune. Theresa, with her patchwork quilt poncho and inseparable Afghan Hound moved in.

Merely living in a different house did not change Theresa's life noticeably. She continued to receive legal supplies of a heroin substitute, physeptone, from her local GP and was still busy with other aspects of the drug culture. Ten days after arriving at Jan's house, she ate a large meal of fish, chips and coca-cola, fell asleep, vomited, inhaled and died. Jan in fact found her while she was still alive, but she was dead by the time she reached hospital. The post mortem showed that she had a medically 'safe' level of physeptone in her bloodstream—a relatively clear day for Theresa.

2: Rebels With A Cause

The death of Theresa Curry was a tragic event and yet strangely creative. My responsibility was to break the news to Theresa's parents.

I first telephoned the director of social services to inform him, because Theresa had been in the care of the local authority. The director, Jim Terry, was immediately supportive. He warned, however, that the parents had previously been very critical of the way Kingston's social services department had exercised its responsibilities towards Theresa. He feared that they might react angrily at the news of her death.

Jim offered to go to see Mr and Mrs Curry himself, but I felt that it really was my duty. On occasions like this a minister must look to God for inspiration. It is hardly possible to rehearse how one will break news of this kind. I felt fairly calm, however, as I drove to the house. I think that directly I entered, we all knew what had happened. It was not therefore too difficult to make the explicit statement.

I was profoundly grateful that the parents immediately assured me that they attributed no blame to Kaleidoscope. Indeed, they expressed appreciation for what we had tried to do and spoke of their daughter's evident happiness during the last few days of her life. We spoke quietly together—it was a sacred occasion.

News spread rapidly among the hippy scene of Theresa's death. The newspapers also made her death public. They were anxious days because Kaleidoscope was not yet well established and we had many critics.

The two houses at 44–46 Cromwell Road had been derelict for some years before Jan, Martin and Richard moved in and formed the first attempt at a hostel. The outward appearance was indeed shabby and no money was available for extensive renovation. Our neighbours therefore were already inclined to believe that the place was not fit for habitation. Indeed at this point an anonymous person sent a letter to the local authority stating that a closure order seemed appropriate.

In these circumstances it was easy to understand why many people regarded the death of Theresa as proof of our absurd incompetence to do serious work with young people whose problems were acknowledged to be complex.

I was also uncertain about the response of church members. I knew that one or two of them wondered if we were really attempting work for which we were not properly skilled. Would this be the point at which the members would say: 'no further'?

Obviously an inquest would need to be held and I dreaded descriptions of the shabby interior of the house, with its broken bannisters and inadequate plumbing. In those days, most of our residents chose to sleep on the floor. In a novel variation of this, Richard constructed what we called the baboon shelf. That is, his bed was suspended a few feet below the ceiling in the corner of the room. Pictures of such sleeping conditions in a local newspaper would confirm the impression that the whole place was a shambles.

I announced the news to the church, which also recognised the seriousness of the situation. We were all in sombre mood.

We arranged the funeral service in two parts; the first

being held in the John Bunyan Baptist Church. The chapel in those days was a typical non-conformist preaching auditorium with pews and a horseshoe shaped gallery facing a vast pulpit. The second part of the service was to be a requiem mass at St Agatha's Roman Catholic Church. We heard that large numbers of hippies intended to come to the services. The Ursuline Convent at Wimbledon also wished to send a large group of pupils and staff. The press rang up to ask what time the services were to be held and asked me if I would care to make a statement. We all sensed that this was going to be a big occasion.

The service at the John Bunyan Church can only be described as a great celebration. The press estimated that 140 hippies were seated in the back pews. In front of them was a large contingent of convent girls, who in those days dressed in a uniform which included straw boaters and white gloves. The nuns who accompanied them were in traditional black habits. Occupying the front pews were representatives from the social services department. Church members and members of Theresa's family also sat at the front. The church was practically full.

It is hard to explain why the service seemed triumphant. I spoke of Theresa's hopes and aspirations and tried to communicate to the general public the positive qualities of the hippy movement; the idealism behind the rejection of materialism and the longing for a true expression of love and peace among all people. It is easy to criticise such fragile optimism and, of course, there were many contradictions within the hippy movement. But it is important not to deny the true spiritual aspirations of many of these young people.

As I preached I sensed that many of the young people present reached out towards the ideals I spoke about; at the same time many of the older people in the congregation listened intently, trying hard to understand and to respond positively to the youthful ideals I spoke of that day. A moment of drama occurred when a middle-aged woman came to the rostrum and declared that it was God's will and Theresa's wish that the work of Kaleidoscope should go forward. She prophesied that new buildings would replace the present ones. I had never experienced anything like this before. We all knew that out of tragedy we could feel the promise of a new beginning.

The requiem mass at St Agatha's was an equally moving event. Father John Cremin, the parish priest, had baptised Theresa as an infant and it seemed appropriate that he should celebrate the mass. For many of the members of the Baptist church, it was the first time they had been present at a requiem mass. Father Cremin expressed a vision of heaven which is not often described in modern Protestant churches. Reading the liturgy, he commended Theresa to God and continued:

'May Mary, the angels and all the saints
come to meet you as you go forth from this life.
May Christ who was crucified for you
bring you freedom and peace.
May Christ, the Son of God, who died for you
take you into his kingdom.
May Christ, the Good Shepherd,
give you a place within his flock.
May he forgive your sins
and keep you among his people.
May you see your Redeemer face to face
and enjoy the sight of God for ever. Amen.'

For many of us it seemed that heaven itself was opened to us. This appreciation of Catholic worship was the beginning of a process which has continued within the John Bunyan Baptist Church since those days.

Something remarkable had fused around the short life of Theresa Curry. A crucifix given by the nuns of her convent still hangs in the Bunyan prayer chapel.

But for the newspapers, the police and some local politicans, the event was confirmation of their worst fears. Theresa, after all, was one of the 'five found dead' whose fate had justified the police attack on Kaleidoscope.

Looking back on that police raid, however, it is evident that it too was a landmark of a different kind; requiring both the police and the wider public to make a decision about Kaleidoscope. Was this an activity to be encouraged or one to be stamped out at the earliest opportunity?

The raid itself took place on a typical Kaleidoscope Friday night, just before the Christmas of 1973. The club was crowded with women in long, exotic dresses made from velvet or embroidered with sequins; men with shoulder length hair. In all, about one hundred people, which for the Isaac Stalberg Hall amounted to a full house.

Pink Floyd, another of those period sounds, was playing—diffuse music; a synthesis of vague reflection with sharp statement. Quiet music, really.

People were talking, drinking coffee. Some certainly were stoned. Most were just happy. I felt relaxed, sitting at a barrel-top table with my back to the door. David Langridge, assistant minister to the church and a local boy, was also there. Tall and thin, David's meticulous style complemented my less than disciplined entrepreneurial approach. Neither of us, however, was equipped to deal with the violence we had often been forced to encounter in the club.

Suddenly, three big men in their 40s rushed into the club. One of them, a thick-set, grim man tried to jump on to a table,upsetting a cup of coffee over a girl as he did so. A group of young Irishmen who were sitting at the table grappled with him and he fell. His two companions sprang to his aid. David and I leapt towards the scene of action.

By now, the room was filling up with policemen. All told, 39 officers and two police dogs took part in the raid. I called for calm and the fluorescent lights were switched on and the music off. We asked to see the police warrant, whereupon the thick-set officer climbed on a table and read the legal document. The two Irishmen who had grappled with him were charged with assault.

The police ordered everyone to stand against the walls to be searched. Names and addresses were taken and some people led outside. After several minutes of uneasy silence, Sam Campbell, the Kaleidoscope joker, called out: 'Is it cool to roll a joint?' There was a roar of laughter and Sam was bundled outside. He was later charged with assaulting the police.

For the most part, people in the club co-operated with the police, which made a series of subsequent charges of obstruction and assault difficult to comprehend. When a policewoman took hold of a young blonde girl, however, the girl, who was emotionally unstable, became hysterical. The policewoman wrenched her to the ground. In court later, the police officer claimed she had been bitten on the leg and produced a photograph in evidence. 'It could have been a love bite,' the defending solicitor told the court.

In many respects, the police raid resembled farce, but there were several very serious aspects. The most alarming came when three police officers went beyond the club building into the adjacent church hall and church. Upstairs, above the church hall, the recently recruited Kaleidoscope doctor had his surgery, where he was offering a comprehensive medical service to a group of people, many of whom were homeless and not registered with a general practitioner. In his work Dr Nick Herrick was assisted by a state registered nurse, Margaret Taylor. The doctor and nurse were at work in the surgery when the police arrived. First the doctor was told to leave and then the nurse was instructed to remove her clothes. She was strip searched—an experience which can only be described as humiliating in the intimacy it involves. Having found nothing, the nurse was then ordered to hand over the Kaleidoscope medical records. She refused, so the police said they would take the files away.

When I saw policemen reappear in the club, carrying a file containing about 90 names, I refused to allow them past the club door. I was told I would be arrested for obstruction if I continued to protest. I thought it best for me to witness what was happening and did not therefore wish to be arrested and taken away. I made a final protest and then telephoned a local magistrate, Ted Curtis, also the borough youth officer, who agreed to come to the club. Meanwhile Margaret had telephoned the Kaleidoscope doctor, who spoke to the police. The file was then returned to the surgery, but police demanded that the nurse read out the names and addresses of all patients. No explanation was given then or later, but it was assumed the police believed they were garnering a comprehensive list of local drug offenders.

Over the next few weeks, Kaleidoscope fought for its reputation. It found some powerful allies when 'Doctor', the family practitioner's newspaper, published a story about the raid, raising questions about the breach of medical confidentiality. The *Guardian* newspaper also took up the issue and Mr Louis Blom-Cooper, the well-known Queen's Counsel, and the National Council of Civil Liberties became involved in challenging the police action.

But Kaleidoscope primarily needed recognition and support in its own community. Gradually, it came. Old friends, such as officials from the town's youth service and social services department, spoke out on Kaleidoscope's behalf—they had seen its work. And the Kingston Council of Churches, in February 1974, publicly put its weight behind Kaleidoscope, when in a statement signed by the chairman, the Rev Keith Fisher, minister of Kingston's United Reformed Church, the council declared: 'This is one of the very few organisations in the borough which attempts, on this scale, to guide and support young people in need, and we believe it deserves the wide encouragement and support of the people of Kingston.'

Relations with the police, however, were at the lowest point imaginable. An official complaint was made, which at first seemed to receive careful consideration. But something like eighteen months then elapsed before we received a dossier setting out the evidence from both sides. It concluded that the police had made only technical errors. Meanwhile a war of attrition continued. Jan was arrested outside her house, on her way to post a letter, and taken to the station and strip searched. Kaleidoscope became actively involved in campaigning against the extent of police powers to stop and search an individual on suspicion of carrying drugs.

Eventually, I decided to take legal action against the police, at which point an opportunity for reconciliation unexpectedly occurred.

A senior officer from the Metropolitan Police sent Mary and me an invitation to lunch and over the meal he told us that he was appointing a liaison officer, Chief Inspector Miss Celia Cundy, whose task would be to resolve problems between the club and the police. Hours were spent listing complaints and agreeing procedures for the future. They would be tested many times.

In 44–46 Cromwell Road, a deep sense of alienation set in. It seemed as if everything the residents did was suspect. The period of The Angry Brigade came, when young intellectuals launched a bombing campaign on 'establishment' targets. Jan's house was searched in the middle of the night for bombs. At other times, police came in search of dead bodies and drugs. It felt to Jan, Richard and Martin, who were now joined by a young, recently married couple, Ian and Liz Hargreaves, as if they were being constantly worked over by the agents of some ring of organised crime. Their response was to publish broadsheets, which joined in the contemporary attack on police powers, whilst in the same publications debating the meaning of eucharist and the plans of property developers who were encroaching ever further into the residential space at the heart of Kingston.

They were sometimes heady, sometimes squalid, depressing days. By now the two houses, 44 and 46, were knocked into one and a communal style of living pursued. The main evening meal of each day was shared; cooking went by turn and cleaning chiefly by default. The houses were in poor condition. The roof leaked, the plumbing did not work and there was no running hot water outside the kitchen. In a magnificent gesture of generosity, someone supplied an electric shower unit, but it never worked properly. These residential volunteers—they shunned the word 'staff'—were paid between £5 and £10 a week. The money came from the local youth service, which in effect paid them for a few hours' youth club work each week.

The idea was that the volunteers would share their lives, their explorations and their problems, with the lives, explorations and problems of a handful of young people who were without homes and wanted to live there.

Many remarkable characters passed through. Some

changed their lives, some barely had time to change their socks.

Cliff and Amy were systematic renegades. They called themselves anarchists and Cliff was a talented graphic artist. Like Jan, North American, they were among the first residents, qualifying chiefly on the grounds of straight homelessness. Cliff, however, was deeply paranoid and saw the agency of the secret police behind the sight of a telephone engineer climbing a nearby telegraph pole. 'Property is theft'—a favourite anarchist slogan—became for a time a principle by which the house tried to live. But Cliff was unable to deal with the self-exposure needed in the communal structure as the group grew larger and eventually Cliff and Amy left.

Most of those who went to live in the house, however, got there by way of the club. Sylvia collapsed one night in the club, in the days before Kaleidoscope had its own surgery. When a doctor was called he gave a rapid diagnosis. 'She is pregnant. She is malnourished. She has chronic bronchitis. She is a drug addict and she has lice. She is not an ambulance case, but she needs care and medical treatment.'

Sylvia lived in the house for a year and was soon joined by her boyfriend Dave. Both were serious narcotics addicts and Dave was violent and unpredictable. When disappointed or resisted, their reactions could be terrible. Dave threatened Martin with a knife. Property was stolen. Sylvia slung a brick through Jan's window, wailing about the political inequality of the growing gulf between 'staff' and the rest.

Pru and Peter arrived one night and begged to be taken in. Pru was Sylvia's closest friend. I visited Pru's parents, as I had visited Sylvia's. Both families were prosperous and totally perplexed about their daughters' lifestyles. Pru's parents, Christian people, were relieved to learn of the whereabouts of their daughter, but hardly reassured. Pru's father visited Cromwell Road, wearing a stiff, bright manner which could not conceal his rapt bewilderment at the conditions his daughter was choosing to live in.

Kaleidoscope offered no formal therapy; only acceptance and security. It seemed at the time better than nothing, although sometimes it was painfully little. At this time I lived two miles away from Kaleidoscope and our family sustained Kaleidoscope volunteers through regular Sunday lunches and afternoon conversations.

I never missed the Friday club and I tried to befriend the young people who came to it. But I felt strongly that anything like preaching would be inappropriate. Christ fed the multitude and presented his message of the kingdom by signs and in parables. That is what I felt we had to do. We would not put up posters about God's creation, we would serve good food and coffee. We would not talk easily of love, we would try the harder way of loving. Everyone was suspicious of authority and of formulaic answers.

On one occasion, I found myself alongside Maureen Murphy. Maureen had a picture of a baby boy at her bedside; she had agreed to the child's adoption, under immense pressure, some years earlier. Now she was pregnant again.

As she cried in her room each night, Maureen felt herself heading for another disastrous episode in her life.

'God is punishing me for my sins,' she told me. 'I want to keep my baby, but they won't let me. They took my last baby away. They'll put him in care if he's not adopted. God *must* be punishing me for my sins.'

'Tell me these things for which you think God is punishing you,' I said. It made a long list. Maureen was inconsolable.

'But look around you here,' I said. 'Jan has shared her house with you and with many others. You have decorated your room. You have chosen these light, happy colours. Martin cooks good food. You will not be forced to give up your baby. We will help you. You have medical care and we will help you with your baby; this is your home.

'But God does not want me to have peace,' said Maureen. 'He is angry. I have done so many wrong things.'

'But Maureen, things are working out better for you now. You are here because God inspired the members of the church to start Kaleidoscope. That shows God loves you. You have the proof of that in this place. God is not punishing you. God forgives and helps you start again.'

I paused to give the girl God's blessing and she smiled. Maureen now lives in Kingston with her son and has since married. She looks a happy, stable woman.

Like Maureen, Sheila Kelly was Irish and not at all connected with the culture of hippies and drugs with which Kaleidoscope was becoming associated. Newly arrived from Ireland with her husband Joe, Sheila was pregnant and the pair sleeping rough by the River Thames. One day, having been refused local authority housing, they arrived on the doorstep of 44–46 Cromwell Road and a room was found for them. They expressed their gratitude in many ways; naming their baby Joe Eric Kelly. Joe Kelly senior also accomplished a mysterious miracle one day, when a shopkeeper donated to the house a large, industrial fridge. The combined efforts of all the residents were not equal to the task of carrying it upstairs to the kitchen, which amused Joe.

'I'll shift it for you,' he said. 'In return for a bottle of sherry.' It was a bargain. 'But I'll be needing a good night's sleep first.'

Next morning, the fridge was there in the kitchen. 'Ah, it wasn't so bad,' said Joe. 'Easy when you know how.'

A year later, Joe revealed his secret to me. On the night in question he had met two Irish navvies and offered to share the bottle with them if they would help him lift the fridge.

By then, Joe and Sheila were living a different life. Kaleidoscope's increasingly close contacts with a local housing association had been put to good effect in finding Joe and Sheila a job in an old people's home. They were popular with the old people, but trouble began when officials received complaints about Joe's drunkenness.

Joe and Sheila both swore that the tales were untrue. Joe liked an occasional drink, but had not been drunk or unsteady since the day they took the job. Eventually, the couple were dismissed and returned to live at Kaleidoscope. Joe found a job with a builder.

Again, things started well, until Joe's boss noticed his new man was unsteady on his feet some days. Joe was sacked a second time.

Later that same day, police called at Cromwell Road to tell Sheila that Joe had been admitted to hospital and was in a coma. I went with Sheila to the hospital, where they were told that Joe had a brain tumour. A week later, he was dead.

Sheila was full of grief and questions. Eventually, I realised there was a question the unhappy woman had not dared to put. 'I think you want to ask me if Joe has gone to heaven,' I said. 'Yes,' replied Sheila, anxiously. 'Sheila,' I said, 'do you think that if I was in charge of admissions to heaven, Joe would be admitted.' 'Oh yes,' she said, 'you understand Joe.' 'But if I understand Joe, surely God understands him even better and certainly loves him more. Joe is in heaven.'

Mostly, though, the residents of the house were youngsters, caught in the cross winds of some insupportable domestic circumstance and looking to their friends and the basic optimism of the youth culture of their time for salvation.

Becky had left a prosperous home and divided parents at the age of 14. At 16, when she arrived at Kaleidoscope, she had seen the worst side of most things, but still wore a vibrant smile, capable of lighting up a room or a conversation. When Des Wilson, who had left Shelter, the housing charity, to become a journalist on the *Observer*, ran a cover story on Kaleidoscope in the newspaper's colour supplement, Becky was the inevitable selection for the cover photograph. She persuaded the newspaper to buy her a new dress for the occasion. Becky was to live out many dramas at Kaleidoscope.

Like Becky, Robin was handsome but adrift. His father worked hard in the City and came home late each day looking for peace and evidence that his family shared his values of ambition and self-assertion. His mother was anxious, a user of prescribed anti-depressants, trying to create the atmosphere her husband wanted.

By the time he was 16, Robin had discovered that barbiturate sleeping pills were easily obtained. Taken at first with a glass of beer, or something stronger, they had a blissfully intoxicating effect. By the time that he was crushing them up and injecting them into his veins, the drugs were capable of reducing him to a permanently shambling gait and total unreliability. His father, desperate to maintain the home in his own self-image, suggested Robin should sleep in the conservatory, so as not to disturb the family peace when he stumbled home in the middle of the night.

Robin also attracted a lot of police attention. His shoulder length black hair and stoned behaviour made him a legitimate stop and search target. Sometimes, he would be searched on the streets four or five times in a single day. Eventually, he found his way from the conservatory, to the streets, to Kaleidoscope.

He did not stay there long. Margaret Taylor, who was the link between Robin and the Kaleidoscope doctor, found his body underneath his bed. A suicide note spoke of his unhappiness at home and was more viciously bitter than Robin could ever have been in speech about his treatment by the police.

The suicide note also thanked Kaleidoscope, where Robin said he had found acceptance. But for the Kaleidoscope staff, it was becoming increasingly obvious that the facilities, buildings and methods of Jan's house were not equal to the task of sustained care for a group of people in such fragile condition. Ian and Liz left the house at this time, feeling that their skills and experience were not sufficiently formed to continue the work. Shortly afterwards, another pair of residents with whom Ian and Liz had shared many struggles gave up. Liam first killed his drug addict girlfriend and then overdosed himself. He had frequently talked and even painted about his dream of dying to a piece of music by the rock group Led Zeppelin. The song was called 'Stairway to heaven'.

3: An Expensive Dream

Plans for rebuilding John Bunyan Baptist Church and the Kaleidoscope Club existed from the earliest days. It was apparent when we first arrived in Kingston in 1968 that the airy, galleried church, which had not been full for decades, was inappropriate to an area which was no longer primarily residential. But the idea of what to build in its place emerged slowly.

The site of the church was undoubtedly valuable. A slice of it was wanted for a road-widening scheme and I set about discovering how we could raise funds, since the church had none, for a major rebuilding scheme.

I contacted a property developer, who was eager for the opportunity to build luxury flats, which would be situated 500 yards from a main commuting station to London and five minutes walk from the river. Out of the profits from the flats, a chapel could be built, with some small additional facilities, perhaps including a club. I was introduced to David Cole, an architect who had just completed a similar scheme for an Anglican Church in Battersea and drawing number one, the first of over a hundred, was begun.

The drawings changed for many reasons. As the church discovered, experimentally and in small groups at first, the attractions of worship in the round, the idea developed of building a round chapel.

Jan, David and Andrea had all come to commitment to Christ when they had been introduced to the breaking of bread. They had therefore a special attachment to the sacrament. Martin had a Roman Catholic upbringing and all of the group of new young people had been influenced to some extent by the mysticism of eastern religions. They therefore reinforced my own preference for holy communion every Sunday—in my own case this stemmed from my earlier associations with the Christian Brethren on the one hand and with the Catholic and Anglican Churches on the other.

This focus upon communion led logically to a central position for the communion table and for seating on four sides.

We had also discovered, in other contexts, the advantages of sitting in a circle. Martin had introduced the custom of holding weekly Ebenezer suppers in the Kaleidoscope club, at which an odd mixture of people would gather. The name was chosen in honour of Ebenezer Clark, a long-dead member of the church whose bequest of £23,000 was one of the few solid financial resources available for the future. At these Ebenezer suppers, individuals would sometimes play a musical instrument or perform some piece of drama and Martin would lead the group, sitting in a circle, in the oriental practice of 'om'—a kind of communal humming which was beyond no one's technical capability and sometimes provoked hilarity, sometimes pleasant contemplation.

The church also established the custom of organising occasional trips to Berlin, which involved visits to both East and West Germany and much political discussion. On one of them, I was invited to the Protestant church at Plotzensee, close to the prison where Hitler hanged the officers who had attempted a rebellion against his dictatorship. Plotzensee prison and the church are both now monuments to the fight against fascism and the persistence of hope in the midst of frightful inhumanity.

But what most caught my imagination, as I sat through a sermon in a language I could not understand, was the fact that I was sitting in a square church, with a communion table in the centre.

This was the arrangement we had considered for our new chapel and here I could see how it worked. I made mental notes on the Plotzensee design's shortcomings—the pulpit was too dominant; the organ protruded too far into the central space and the communion table ought not to have been mounted on a plinth. I could hardly wait to get back to Kingston to communicate these observations to David Cole. He quickly produced drawings based on our previous discussion and my fresh impressions.

It was the same with the luxury flats. Jan and the others did not like the idea of building expensive accommodation on a site where they were now offering free places for people with nowhere else to go. Gradually, the idea of a hostel replaced the flats proposal and I set out to discover how other organisations, like the YMCA, managed to finance such projects.

There was also long debate about the style of the hostel. The group then living in Cromwell Road liked the eccentricities of Victorian architecture. There was little enthusiasm for a modern building. I tried to tease out some of the fears about new buildings.

There was the fear of too much uniformity because of restricted budgets. Most hostels have rectangular rooms of standard size situated on both sides of a corridor. There was also the fear that residents would live isolated lives secure in their own bedsits. The community life which was a feature of the old house might easily disappear.

One day, discussing these fears the child of one of the residents in the old house said: 'New buildings don't have corners.' This remark was the clue to resolving many of our problems. I immediately communicated the comment to David Cole and asked him to design irregular shaped bedrooms clustered around common rooms and kitchens to ensure that the communal lifestyle continued to flourish. The common rooms, we decided, should also have fireplaces. These features were all incorporated into the final design, with great success.

Another clear requirement was a small reception area where a member of staff could be on duty at all times. This would avoid the intolerable burden of the member of staff living nearest to the front door being permanently on call. This in turn led to the question of the degree of separation between staff and other residents and the need for greater privacy. All these points were thrashed out on the basis of a mounting body of practical experience.

On the question of catering there was agreement that the vegetarian style which had developed in the old house should continue, but people disagreed whether we should employ a single cook or continue to take turns at preparing the meals.

As these issues were turned over, the drawings submitted to the town planning department were turned down. Kaleidoscope was a name which still attracted great hostility from many councillors and residents. It took six years to overcome these difficulties with a mixture of planning, lobbying, public debate and constant effort to make Kaleidoscope better understood and accepted. Indispensable help in this process came from Mr Jim Terry, director of social services, and Miss Angela Julia, his deputy, who had almost from the beginning recognised the value of a service which, even in sub-standard accommodation, was offering a service not available elsewhere in the borough. This backing was maintained, with considerable courage, through casualties, errors and shortcomings.

When planning permission eventually came, it was for a

35-room, four-storey hostel, with car parking in the basement. Across a cobbled square, intended to form the first half of an ultimate quadrangle in a phase two development, there would be a square chapel, linked to a small prayer chapel and office. Above the chapel, provision was made for a community hall and below it, in the basement, for the Kaleidoscope club and medical facilities.

But it was still not clear where the £500,000 needed to build it would be found. The Housing Act had created a legal framework for housing associations to borrow money from the Department of the Environment, to be paid back over 60 years from rents. So the Kaleidoscope (Kingston) Housing Association was formed to raise a loan of £300,000.

The remaining £200,000 came from an assortment of sources. The Department of Education and Science was persuaded to make a grant of £18,000 for the club and a by now more sympathetic local authority came up with £9,000. £60,000 was raised by the strategem of the church selling to the Kaleidoscope (Kingston) Housing Association the portion of the church's freehold land on which the hostel would be built. The piece of land needed for road widening was worth £30,000 and the Department of Health and Social Security offered £9,000 for the medical work. And then there was Ebenezer Clark's bequest—£23,000. That still left £50,000.

These were big numbers for a church treasurer used to collecting a weekly offering of £50. There was no alternative, however, but to sell the church's only remaining piece of real estate—its manse, without which members feared it would be difficult to attract a possible successor to myself. It also meant that Mary and I, along with our three teenage children, would have to move into the hostel. The manse was sold for £18,000.

Although the numbers still did not quite add up, building work began. There were small donations and endless efforts to raise money through an annual charity shop and other activities. After the demolition men had completed their work, the Kaleidoscope club was held in the site hut, which was neatly designed so that site regulation notices could be reversed on Friday nights to display posters more suitable for the club atmosphere.

With its red gingham curtains, the building site club was a considerable success, although it was not able to offer either the space or facilities to be provided in the planned buildings. But it established continuity. Church services were transferred to a nearby Anglican vicarage, which had been vacated pending yet another road development.

But faster than additional money could be raised, building costs rose. At one meeting of the church deacons—the lay members elected by the church to assist the minister—I reported another round of increased costs. Michael Dale, a deacon of many years standing, remarked: 'Well, we can't have only half a roof.' In such a spirit, the church swallowed its anxieties and trusted a vision. Building work continued and every day I was on site, discussing details with the site foreman and architect.

4: Embers

Just before the demolition gang moved on to the site, Kaleidoscope had another moment of high drama.

It was just turned midnight in the club in the spring of 1975. Packed into the club that Friday was a familiar crowd; the atmosphere still had a strong whiff of the 1960s, but leather jackets and blue jeans were taking over from the more individualistic and colourful styles of a few years earlier.

But there was still no shortage of individuals. One boy, tall, skinny and resolutely anonymous, had been in the club most Fridays that winter, dressed only in a loin cloth. John and Leo were at the bar, staring into their drugged selves. Becky was there, wearing a leather miniskirt which could not fail to attract attention. She was with her most faithful companion, Noel. It was a happy night, the kind which experience had taught us all too often could be a smokescreen for trouble.

Four men I had never seen before entered the club. They had purposeful expressions. The oldest one was perhaps a little over 30. The other three, I guessed, were in their late twenties.

The older man wore a stylish, tan coloured leather jacket and had a confident, almost relaxed and pleasant manner. His three companions, however, were less reassuring. They wore three-quarter length coats, under which they carried yard-long iron bars, deliberately only partly concealed.

It was immediately obvious that the men were recognised

by many of the people in the club. Conversation subsided, except that some of the young men in the club tried to appear to be on easy terms with the group. Then people began to move towards the older man, and the three-man bodyguard let them approach.

I signalled to David and we both moved in to investigate. The older man stood in our way. We soon saw what was happening, however. The older man was openly selling orange and blue capsules of a barbiturate drug, Tuinal. He had a canister about eight inches long containing hundreds of pounds worth of the drug.

I immediately protested, although I dared not push any of the bodyguards out of the way. 'We don't allow dealing in the club.' I decided that on this occasion I must try to remember descriptions to give to the police.

The men at first ignored my warning, but then the central figure said in measured speech: 'I wouldn't interfere if I were you.' His assistants turned to face me and they gripped their iron bars menacingly.

I felt sick. I had seen the victims of violence. I had no time to pray. 'I have no alternative but to telephone the police,' I said as firmly as I could, although I am sure it sounded nervous. I moved towards the telephone, expecting any moment to feel my head split open.

'That's exactly what you'll do if you want your place burned down,' one of the men called out. I forced my index finger into the nine of the telephone dial. I was acting automatically, doing my task without thinking of the consequences. I dialled nine—nine—nine.

I tried to calm my voice and hurried through the obligatory questions and answers with the operator. I gave my name, address, telephone number and urgent request to the police. I dropped the receiver back onto its rest and turned to see what was happening.

Many of the people in the club were looking wretchedly towards me. They seemed to be sharing my agony.

The men made no move towards me. They carried on as if nothing unexpected was happening, as if they were playing out what to them was an already written script—for the benefit of their clients. It seemed as if they had perfectly calculated the time the police would take to arrive.

A few minutes later, they strode out of the club, as audaciously as they had entered it. As they left, one of them stepped aside and said to me in everyone's hearing. 'You heard what we said. It's a pity you wouldn't listen. You have a nice place here.' They walked out into the night, as if they had simply made a business call on a customer who had defaulted on his payments.

The police arrived a few minutes later and wrote down descriptions of the men. One police officer asked another if they should search the place, but they decided not to bother. Without saying goodnight, they climbed back into the car and were gone.

Some days later, we were excited by a telephone call from Bob Searchfield, head of the Standing Conference on Drug Abuse—a Government-funded organisation which represented and co-ordinated some of the work of voluntary organisations concerned with the problems of drug abuse.

Searchfield explained that in the past two years, a group of experts had, under the auspices of the United Nations, studied different approaches to dealing with drug abuse and were moving in favour of a community approach. They were uncertain precisely how to define such an approach, and in particular they were pondering whether a community facility could succeed if it were attached to a hospital. The panel had already visited several medical-based projects in Britain and was anxious to see something different. Kaleidoscope had been suggested.

I delighted in this kind of occasion. I love to talk about our work and to submit ideas to others for discussion. And Kaleidoscope was at a stage where the endorsement of a prestigious international panel could be crucial in unlocking the capital still needed to construct the new buildings and then to provide a secure revenue base to run them.

The rest of the week was one of painstaking preparation. The club was cleaned and partly repainted. Toilets, the bane of any club because of the constant graffiti they attract, not to mention the uncertainties of ancient plumbing, would have to sparkle.

At this point, there were few Kaleidoscope staff on hand, because 44–46 Cromwell Road were on the point of demolition. Jan and Martin had departed on a trip to India, from where Jan would return to her native Canada to become, eventually, a social worker. Richard, having long ago renounced the impulses which took him to study modern languages at Cambridge, was training as a carpenter and had moved to Wales with his new wife Bridget.

So most of the burden fell on church members, who at that point numbered around 30. In particular Alan Roberts, the church secretary, and his wife Uschi engaged their formidable energies.

Alan is an engineer—a man more comfortable with action than words and Uschi is a wonderful cook. Their talents were precisely what was needed as I concentrated on preparing a paper for the seminar: 'An attempt to achieve the social integration of drug users and the prevention of abuse in Kingston-upon-Thames.' It was to be given before lunch on April 15.

By midnight on April 14, every detail was perfect. David and I surveyed the club. It had never looked better.

At 4.30 am, the police telephoned me to say that the club

was on fire and I was needed at the site. The drug dealers' promise had been kept. As I watched the twisting steel girders, I knew there was no hope of saving so much as a stick of furniture.

'We have a team from the United Nations due here in six hours time,' I said to a policeman watching the blaze.

'They'll have to hurry up if they want to see the last embers,' he said.

How could the visit go ahead? The obvious way was to beg charity of a neighbouring church and borrow a church hall or even, since several VIPs were also due to attend, to ask the local authority for use of the Guildhall.

'We can't do that,' I said to Mary. 'It will mean serving instant coffee in plastic cups. How can we bring this thing alive in the Guildhall?'

Inspiration struck. Kaleidoscope had just inherited from Kingston Parish Church the vicarage, which was to be used as a makeshift place of worship for the church. At present it was unoccupied, neglected and overgrown; but it was a handsome, spacious house, not far from the burned-out club. The challenge appealed to me and I sensed the opportunity to carry the event off in a style which would give us self-confidence.

At 5.30 am I telephoned Alan and Uschi. Ten minutes later, Alan was at the vicarage, sorting things out. Jack Rance, a church member for many years, said he would loan a sitting room carpet and transport as much furniture as possible. Ted Curtis, the Borough Youth Officer, who could always be relied upon in a crisis, appeared with a Land Rover. Sally and Tony Murray, two volunteers who helped at the Friday club, responded immediately to the call for help. With the aid of the small number of staff then employed by the project—David and his wife Fran, along with Ian Fairbairn, another young graduate just out of university—this small team set out to clean, furnish and make ready the vicarage.

Since much of the food prepared for the visit had also gone up in smoke, I telephoned church members to ask if any had Christmas puddings in store—they would be a novelty for visitors from overseas.

We needed more furniture and I telephoned the night staff at Bentalls, the large department store in the centre of Kingston, and asked for permission to select goods for the visit before the store opened. At 8 am, I was inside the store, with an early duty manager, and 90 minutes later my shopping was completed. The manager was uncertain whether delivery could be made by 10.30, but he would do his best. 'But how do you propose to pay, sir?' he asked.

A few moments later, the store manager reappeared. 'I'm sorry, sir, your bank is unwilling to honour this cheque.'

The bank manager, ignorant of the circumstances, had obviously baulked at a cheque for such a large amount. Alan was called, saw the situation was hopeless and persuaded me to back off. It would be best, he said, to ask church members to bring any food they could, as soon as possible. When we reached the vicarage, empty-handed, we found that most of the work was in fact taken care of. Christmas puddings were being boiled in the kitchens of an old people's home, Uschi was cooking, human chains were moving chairs from the pavement to the house and inside, the vicarage was looking handsome. The grass had been cut.

When the UN coach arrived, exactly on time at 10.30 am, I was standing beside a smouldering building, wearing my best suit and a welcoming expression which sat oddly against the background. As he opened the coach door, Bob Searchfield looked as if he had stumbled upon the holocaust itself.

I mounted the coach and explained the events of the last 12 hours. The programme, I said, would go on as planned, except that the party was invited to survey the burned-out site, simply to familiarise themselves with its location. I was playing for a little time and continued to do so by then guiding the coach round Kingston's notorious one-way system, adding another 15 minutes to a journey which would have taken five minutes at a stroll. When they arrived at the vicarage gate, they found the inevitable Becky, laughing at the fate of the club.

But the sense of adversity overcome was oxygen to me. The very circumstances of the crisis and the response to it, underlined the community-based nature of Kaleidoscope's efforts.

The talk went well. I spoke of Schumacher's concept of 'homecoming' and said: 'At Kaleidoscope, we are trying to return to basic ideas about living, with an emphasis upon "farmhouse" food, authentic decoration and fittings and simple, unostentatious hospitality. We have the conviction that people need a place they can return to, where they are sure of acceptance and warmth, where the only condition attached to their welcome is that they are not intent on destroying the place. Homecoming has sacred connotations. We all need places where we can find warmth and acceptance whatever our failures and where we can live out our fantasies, where we are safe and under only the most natural restraints. Kaleidoscope is such a place.'

The paper also set out our ideas on dealing with drug abuse. Drug taking, I explained, is a social activity which occurs among people who find life frustrating, unexciting and unhappy. 'We need to provide a more reassuring environment for people to grow up in.

'This needs a radical change in our society so that we experience more gaiety and less competition; so that human needs receive more opportunities for fulfilment and less opportunities for exploration; so that people can find a natural and easy course rather than be channelled along artificial lines.

'These grand objectives cannot be achieved immediately and

a beginning has to be made with modest community projects. Kaleidoscope attempts to be such a project. A community project can achieve more in terms of the prevention of drug abuse and the social reintegration of drug users than clinics and rehabilitation centres.'

Lunch was then served in a freshly mown English garden on a perfect spring day. The ham and cold meats, freshly sliced by Emlyn Skinner, a church member and grocer. The cheese was excellent and English. And the coffee, which I consider a sure sign of the quality of an establishment, was freshly ground and served in real cups. Christmas pudding, not traditional at April garden parties, turned out to be a popular novelty. Everyone cheered when the brandy was lit.

In the afternoon, Kaleidoscope staff were questioned about the effectiveness of their approach to drug abuse. Were they succeeding in addressing, in a complex-free fashion, the whole needs of drug abusers, from homelessness to employment, as well as direct medical needs? It was evident from the shape of the discussion that Kaleidoscope had, through its birth pangs in the now-destroyed club and in Jan's house, fumbled its way towards a simple, optimistic Christian approach to a problem which struck many chords with a sophisticated group of professionals. When the UN report appeared, Kaleidoscope's approach was given warm endorsement. The UN, among its other responsibilities, is the main international agency charged with co-ordinating efforts against illegal drug production, trafficking and abuse. The project had, at last, won confirmation for its efforts from the world at large.

5: Growing Pains

The opening of the new John Bunyan Baptist Church and Kaleidoscope Club on January 22, 1977, was a moment we had lived for. Both Mary and I love great celebrations and we were intent that the style of the day would match the excellence of the buildings which, now they were complete, were generally thought to be a considerable success.

Although from the outside stark and fortress-like in style to give a sense of security, inside the courtyard the brick, four-storey buildings have a pleasing simplicity. The hostel, utilitarian in style in order to contain costs, nevertheless reflects the homecoming theme. Common rooms, around which individual rooms are clustered, have fireplaces. Across the courtyard, the copper-roofed church, with its bell-tower and stained glass, offers a more striking and more original architectural vision.

The centrepiece of the basement club, whose dark green walls are decorated now with artwork by Kaleidoscope residents, is a bright red Aga cooker. The two medical surgeries have hessian walls and floral, art nouveau screens.

But the most remarkable part of the complex is the chapel. An irregular, eight-sided structure with a low-slung cruciform ceiling made from buffed concrete creates in practice a square layout. Bare pine pews, remade by Richard from the original pews of the old church stand on four sides. In each corner stands an element crucial to the pattern of worship; organ, open baptistry, minister's bench and lectern. The church is lit naturally by tall, narrow slit windows and, on one side, by a pair of stained glass windows by John Hayward. They depict the theme of Pilgrim's Progress; the struggle from imprisonment and despair to the golden city.

Other details have been added as the church has developed. A painting by Myfanwy Franks, Kaleidoscope's first resident artist. A flight of terracotta angels made by Victor Bryant. Adjoining the main church is a tiny, dark prayer chapel, where communion is celebrated most weekdays. It is there that the crucifix in memory of Theresa Curry hangs.

The day of the opening was a jamboree. Mr George Thomas MP, then Speaker of the House of Commons, and a companion of mine many years earlier during a fact-finding mission to Angola, conducted the official opening. The Rev Dr Ernest Payne, vice-president of the Baptist Union, and a past president of the World Council of Churches, preached.

Mr Thomas spoke passionately of the 'debt of honour'—£21,000—still outstanding to pay for the buildings and appealed to those present to make sure it was paid. By this point, however, another £2,000 had been donated by singer George Harrison's Material World Foundation. A cluster of youths hung round the church all day hoping that the ex-Beatle would appear, but he did not.

By the end of that tumultuous weekend, over 1,000 people had passed through the buildings. Mary and I slipped away from the elation and the tributes to our vision and fortitude for a few days' holiday; ready to return for the next Sunday's worship.

On our return, we entered the courtyard to find Fran, Dave's wife, a warm, strong-hearted woman but with a nervous manner, in tears. The club had not been cleaned from the previous Friday night's session—a most unusual thing, especially since staff numbers had by now been strengthened in readiness for the build-up of activities.

'What's going on?' I asked. 'Why is everything left so dirty?'

'Don't go on about it to Dave,' sobbed Fran, 'there has already been a terrible row between Dave and Alan.

The blow-up between Alan, never a man to suffer sloppiness gladly, and Dave was the froth on the surface of a murky pool of problems. When I eventually spoke with Dave, I was told that staff were unhappy with my emerging management style. Dave, anxious to avoid the appearance of leading a rebel faction, offered to resign.

It was the most devastating moment in my ministry at Bunyan. Insecure in myself at the thought of moving, with the family, from a private house to the open walls of the hostel, I was already deeply anxious. I was suddenly faced with losing my only long-serving member of staff, Dave, who was also the only person with experience of residential work. It soon became clear also that two other members of a six-man team were in sympathy with Dave's point of view.

The roots of the problem went deep. I had never done residential work and had been only an involved spectator as Jan and the others had wrestled with their communal lifestyle in Cromwell Road. At that time I had sometimes been accused of foisting problems on residential staff I would not tolerate in my own home.

Those days had also left a hopeful but confusing mixture of democratic ideas. At one time, every resident in the house had an equal say in every decision, including who should be admitted to the house. Inevitably, the residents chose to protect their own interests, above all. The models, such as they were, were those of the anarchistic commune and the one member one vote democracy of the Baptist church meeting.

This could and did lead to absurdity. On one occasion, when a piano needed moving to the project, there was a lengthy debate about the matter. Was the piano needed? Was it consistent with the community's views about wastage of resources and simple lifestyles to move it in a motorised vehicle? Could a piano trolley be used to hump it across two miles of pavement? Although part of me loved this striving for the ideal and passion for conversation, another part felt that we had to get on with the job of setting up a really useful community project. Alan became my guardian angel for 'getting on with the job'. Jan first, then others until finally Dave felt that this approach sometimes threatened what they saw as the purity of the enterprise.

The slide into a crisis of management was also precipitated by the very change in physical circumstances. In the early days, staff were paid as youth club officers by the borough of Kingston and residents supported themselves from social security payments. Richard kept any available communal cash in a box in his room, but there was never more than a few pounds. Martin, over six foot tall and dressed in an old fur coat, would push a pram into Kingston market to obtain vegetables, free if he could get them at the end of the day's trading.

Such was the identification of Kaleidoscope at that time with the values of 'the alternative society' that members of one important committee in the borough council argued against financial support for the project on the grounds that they were sure I would reject money from an establishment source.

David was no anarchist, nor by 1977 was the alternative society much talked about. But Dave did feel that it would be wrong to create a hierarchy of command in the project. He suspected that I was setting myself up as a director figure, remote from routine and menial tasks. He criticised the concept of apportioning special responsibilities; so that one individual would be mainly responsible for cooking; another for the accounts and so on. A flashpoint was reached when it came to constructing a detailed rota for the 24-hour manning of the new hostel's reception desk. I announced that I would not be included in this rota. Dave felt this was a violation of the democratic principle which lay at the heart of the Baptist way of life, into whose ministry he had been ordained.

There were also points of style at issue. Dave, temperamentally, cared little for the pomp and circumstance of an opening day and treated the whole business with the casualness he felt it deserved. For me it was a chance to perform; to spread the message more broadly and to achieve recognition.

A staff meeting was held to thrash the matter out. Before it, I had held anxious consultations, with Alan and others and decided I could not avoid making a stand. Now custodian of hundreds of thousands of pounds of public money, I had to take direct responsibility. The final sum of money used to pay the builders had also been borrowed against the security of my own property—a house in Wales I had bought when my own house near Kingston was sold.

'I can no longer agree to important financial decisions being taken by a show of hands at a staff meeting, consisting in the main of young graduates who have no experience of running an organistion. Our turnover is now almost £150,000 a year,' I said.

I was unhappy at the bitterness of the clash and uneasy about the clarity with which I had been forced to choose between a loose, easygoing management style and a more formal approach. I now officially became Director of the project, responsible to a small management committee of the Kaleidoscope Housing Association, whose members included a number of leading local figures. As minister of the church, I was also responsible to the church meeting.

The ghosts of those early struggles have never been completely vanquished. Perhaps it is inevitable in any organisation that there will be some struggle for position, but the pattern established in 1977 of a weekly staff meeting and allocated responsibilities has continued with no major changes. The aim is to secure consensus, but final decisions about major matters are mine. The project today has 17 full-time staff and a similar number of volunteers. Five people are needed to staff the reception area. There is an administrator, George Short. A psychiatrist and two nurses are responsible for the medical unit. One individual co-ordinates the project's growing education unit and there is a full-time artist. There has always been an assistant minister—at present the holder of that position is my daughter, Adele, who was ordained in 1984. Other posts carry responsibility for training and catering. All staff receive the same pay—at present £5,400 a year. The management committee operates with a light hand and is responsible only for major strategic decisions, which are taken in most cases according to my advice or that of George Short, the administrator, who is now the longest serving member of staff apart from myself and Mary.

6: Hooked

In its new buildings, Kaleidoscope worked hard to defend its open, tolerant style and to maintain the confidence of government agencies and professionals that its methods worked and were worth backing.

The 'community approach to drug abuse' which had lit up that springtime seminar with the UN was easier to talk about than to accomplish, but by 1978, Kaleidoscope had ten years of experience and a service of growing sophistication. This did not mean that either the controversy or the problems were over.

In the late 1970s, newspapers forgot about drug abuse. The figures for registered drug addiction started to stabilise and it looked as if the worst was over.

They were years of consolidation for Kaleidoscope, during which the medical work evolved under the direction of a series of doctors. When Dr Herrick treated barbiturate addicts in the old club, he attracted criticism from other doctors, who felt he was making these drugs available too freely. Kaleidoscope held out for its right to apply its by now substantial experience of the problems of drug abusers in the way it felt best. But when Dr Herrick finally left Kaleidoscope it looked as if it might be hard to find another doctor willing to take an all-night clinic dealing with difficult cases and facing possible censure from the medical establishment.

Following a period of bad publicity over the police raid and other incidents which provoked headlines such as

'MINISTER DENIES DRUG RING' and 'REV SPEAKS FOR KNIFE BOY', a woman psychologist decided to visit the club unannounced one Friday night. She stayed for several hours and spoke to many of the people present. Afterwards, she wrote a letter to the local newspaper praising the club and giving her opinion that it provided exactly the kind of support many young people needed.

More important, she contacted her nephew, urging him to visit Kaleidoscope. Dr John Wright visited shortly afterwards and soon agreed to take on the work of the Friday night surgery.

Dr Wright was a young man who liked a challenge. He believed it to be a Christian duty to serve underprivileged people and he had previously worked in church mission hospitals in black townships in South Africa.

At the time, the main drugs of addiction were amphetamines—stimulants, capable of enabling users to stay active and high for periods of days. Dr Wright devoted himself to the treatment of these addicts and gave papers on his methods to medical audiences. His work soon won recognition from some quarters and the reputation of Kaleidoscope was enhanced. John Wright later became a consultant physician and returned to his native South Africa.

Dr Marrek Gawel was a senior registrar when he took over from John Wright and he too was to become a consultant. A neurologist, his special knowledge proved to be of particular benefit to one girl in the hostel who had an embarrassing problem. Angela became a Christian while in the hostel and felt a call to become a nun. Her problem was bed-wetting, which had been attributed by doctors to suppressed anger. A violent childhood, during which she had been beaten by her father, had certainly left her angry—

but she believed that following her conversion she had overcome this resentment. But her bed-wetting continued—causing her deep distress.

Dr Gawel discovered that in fact her incontinence had a neurological cause, almost certainly related to the physical attacks she had suffered as a child, and treated her successfully.

Paul, a barbiturate addict, told Dr Gawel that he started to use the drug to control heart palpitations when under stress. The doctor examined him and then referred him to a heart surgeon, who was able successfully to treat him. Paul's parents, who had previously been antagonistic towards Kaleidoscope, became enthusiastic supporters.

When Dr Gawel moved on to become a professor at a Canadian university, Dr James Close, a young general practitioner, took over. Dr Close served only for a brief period in the late 1970s, when the numbers of drug users again started to grow very rapidly. Dr Close referred many of these to the nearest drug dependency unit, but very few kept their hospital appointments. It was evident that Kaleidoscope needed to achieve more formal recognition as a centre for the treatment of drug dependents. Kaleidoscope therefore decided that it needed to appoint a psychiatrist to develop this work. An advertisement was placed in the medical press.

A handful of doctors applied, but one stood out; Dr T S Nathan—a quietly spoken Indian, patient, with a good sense of humour and, crucially, with enough knowledge of hospitals to see the advantages of a community-based approach.

'Our idea is to bring the hospital to the clients,' I told Dr Nathan at interview.

'That is right,' said the doctor, whose work in psychiatry had given him wide experience of adolescent and drug problems. 'It is also important not to look for motivation in addicts. In my view, the Brain Committee was right. It is better to prescribe drugs for addicts in order to prevent them buying on the black market. Only then do you have a chance to start making progress.'

Dr Nathan's views, reflecting the 1965 Brain Committee report, were then the standard wisdom on the subject. But in the early 1980s, a new wave of narcotic drugs started to flow into western Europe—a result, international police agencies said, of rich Iranians extracting their capital from their country following the Islamic revolution in 1979. With heroin back on the streets again at low prices, drugs again started to hit the headlines. Social sniffing of heroin—'chasing the dragon'—regained popularity and the media was thick with stories about schoolchildren being offered supplies of heroin for as little as £5 a fix. There were also some celebrated casualties—the son of actor Joss Ackland among them—and renewed concern in Government.

It was good for Kaleidoscope that there had been three relatively quiet years, before the debate about 'maintenance versus withdrawal' of addicts crashed back into the open.

At Kaleidoscope, two things were obvious. That it was no good trying to prosecute drug abusers out of their habits and equally pointless expecting them to keep hospital appointments. The first step had to be some kind of stability and acceptance for the drug user. A boy like Robin needed to know that he was accepted when covered in his own vomit and unable to stand, as well as when he was performing to his parents' expectations at school.

Kath arrived at the hostel one day, barefoot, dressed in a fringed garment of soft reds and blues and wearing an emerald silk shawl over her fragile shoulders. She carried a large, patterned Indian bag and a scent of sandalwood emanated from her. She had pale skin, long auburn hair and green eyes. Kath epitomised the past era of the flower children. She was the child of addicts and was destitute and in despair.

We took her in and she settled in quickly, transforming her room into an exotic Eastern tent. Shawls and Indian cloths were draped across ceilings and walls, the light level was low and joss sticks perfumed the air. In the day, Kath worked for the parks department, but in the evenings and at weekends, she was taking drugs to fill the void in her life. She became alternatively melancholy and exalted.

Myfanwy, our project artist, succeeded over a period of months in getting close to her, thus enabling a truthful, if painful encounter to take place. Terrified of being asked to leave, Kath asked Myfanwy into her room. Her speech was slurred and her manner hysterical. 'I know what you're thinking, but I haven't any drugs here—I don't take drugs—you must believe me.'

'I don't believe you,' replied Myfanwy. 'Of course you take drugs, you're a drug addict. We're not going to evict you. We accept you Kath, but we want to help you and we can only do that if you're honest with us and yourself.'

Kath needed to know both the security of her place in the hostel and the understanding of the staff. Assured of these she agreed to a supervised programme of medication. It wasn't easy for her and many nights she sobbed in despair. But gradually her self-confidence and self-esteem grew. She met a boy who helped her to overcome her habit completely. They are now married, living happily in the West Country with a baby son.

When new members of staff arrive, I set out Kaleidoscope's basic approach.

'It is impossible to prevent drug abuse, since there is a vast range of substances which can be abused. The mental states which lead to drug abuse have been with mankind since people first experienced pain.

'Obviously drug trafficking needs to be stopped as much as possible and we leave no one in any doubt about the dangers of drug abuse. But there is no easy way out. From the people we see here, probably 30 per cent of drug addicts cannot find the strength to face life without drugs. Our view is that as a Christian community, we cannot leave them to die, simply because they will not accept regimes of detoxification and rehabilitation. We accept people as they are. That is our starting point.'

In Dr Nathan's early days, the right to offer maintenance prescriptions had to be fought for against health service bureaucracy. Because Dr Nathan was a psychiatrist with a hospital attachment, Kingston's family practitioner committee ruled that he could not issue NHS prescriptions from his surgery. But unless he was able to offer free prescriptions, the doctor could not do his job in the Kaleidoscope surgery.

I appealed to the committee and argued that since Kaleidoscope had 35 beds and employed both a doctor and a nurse, it could be classified as a hospital. An ingenious, but unsuccessful argument. Kingston's Member of Parliament was brought into the problem and made representations; two years of lobbying followed and eventually, it was agreed that Kaleidoscope could be declared an annexe to the official drug dependency unit at the West Middlesex Hospital. During those two years, prescription costs were paid for from church collections.

Kaleidoscope at last had the tools to do the job in the way it thought best. Contact was maintained with the drug scene at street level through the club; immediate problems could be dealt with at the Friday surgery. At the same time, Kaleidoscope was able, with the help of Government funding, to set up a daily collection point for maintenance doses for addicts in the community. In this way, a wide range of drug abusers was brought into contact with the Kaleidoscope community; its religious life, its educational activities, its accommodation, its club, its food and its conviction that all human life is to be equally cherished.

Kaleidoscope has got to know hundreds of drug users through these channels. Their stories are as different from each other as any other set of human stories.

Chloe is a well-spoken, educated girl in her 20s who had a good job at the BBC and caring parents. But when her boyfriend died, a conscious sense of grief and desperation connected with some deeper wish for self-obliteration in her personality made her turn to heroin.

She had told her mother, who brought her to Kaleidoscope in desperation, that she could not help her addiction; playing to the popular notion of the innocent victim hooked by the merciless drug. At Kaleidoscope, she was able to confess at least some of the truth—her anger and dismay at the fact that everyone, even those who loved her, expected her to get over the death of her boyfriend quickly and efficiently.

In a Victorian melodrama, Chloe might have hanged herself, but suicide takes courage and is anonymous in a big city where a death goes almost unnoticed. In any case, suicide would only satisfy a wish to die and her feelings included the need to express anger.

Chloe had rapidly learned how to misuse drugs; persuading a reluctant addict to inject her. It is not easy to inject yourself and addicts find it as distasteful as anyone else. Injection is a deliberately selected obscenity. The penetration of the flesh by the needle and the satisfaction when the drug enters the bloodstream has a certain sexual appeal. Fixing can mark a transition from the innocence of being drug free or simply playing with drugs to a consummation and commitment with a drug habit to the point of death.

At Kaleidoscope, Chloe was saved from the personal disintegration which would have occurred if she had continued to live on the streets in a circle of drug dealers. She has a room of her own in the hostel, good food and a medically prescribed level of drugs. Her general health and self-respect have greatly improved.

Because of her own experience, Chloe could understand Don's addiction to crime. Don had committed offences continuously since childhood and had been in custody of one type or another since the age of 14. When he arrived at Kaleidoscope, he was 24 and a hardened criminal. Don had about him a certain angry shyness, which made him avoid eye contact. The two were quickly attracted to each other.

Eventaully, Chloe and Don made a pact. He would not commit more crime if she would no longer take illegal drugs. For a few weeks, they kept their word to each other, until Chloe returned to the hostel stoned. Don walked out and committed a burglary, was arrested and sent to prison.

When Don came out of prison, Kaleidoscope staff agreed to have him back in the hostel, creating an opportunity for a further bond between him and Chloe. More mature now, Chloe slowly reduced her intake of methadone and the two made plans to find a flat to live in. By the summer of 1985, almost two years after entering the Kaleidoscope hostel, Chloe was drug free.

Other cases are less transigent. Geoff, an Irishman, is in his late 30s and has been an addict for 17 years. The roots of his addiction are lost in memory, but as a young man and a drifter, he had supported his craving for drugs with many desperate expedients. On sixteen occasions, he entered hospitals, put on a white coat and posed as a medical student, before raiding the operating theatre drugs cabinet. Geoff then turned his attention to chemists's shops; before long his life was built around criminal activities associated with his drug abuse.

His body wrecked, Geoff's family decided to take him to England in the belief that he would find treatment, but he proved incapable of detoxification—the main option offered by hospitals. Geoff's brother happened one day to see me on a television broadcast, speaking about Kaleidoscope's maintenance approach. He put Geoff in the car and travelled across London to the hostel. Geoff now makes this same trip—around 30 miles—each day to receive prescribed liquid methadone. He no longer lurches, has much improved general health and is stable. He has started to think about things other than drugs, although it may be years before he can contemplate for himself the idea of giving up drugs. But at least he has been spared some years of pain and the community has been saved from some criminal acts.

Kaleidoscope's system of dispensing drugs has evolved over the years, to deal with the practicalities of addicts' lives. At first, daily prescriptions were issued in tablet form, and patients had to swallow their dose in front of a member of staff. Then it was found that some patients managed to stick the tablets to chewing gum on their back teeth, preserving a half dissolved tablet which could later be sold on the black market.

The answer was methadone in liquid form; unpopular with some addicts at first but effective and controllable. One addict complained that having once almost drowned as a child, he had great difficulty in swallowing liquids. Would Kaleidoscope make an exception and give him pills? Another claimed liquid methadone caused spots.

Eventually, both the core of 35 addicts who visit

Kaleidoscope each day and the Home Office were satisfied. These addicts look like any other string of people arriving for appointments. Some come in cars, some have families and their own children, some have jobs, some do not.

Gordon is an addict who comes daily for his methadone. He is also the father of Sarah, a shy, curly haired two year old. Being a widower is not easy, but being an addict as well makes his life harder still. Gordon is determined that Sarah should not be taken away from him and there is a real bond between them. Stabilised by our medication programme and supported by our playgroup staff, who look after Sarah in the week, he is keeping a home together for them both.

Jean is a pretty fair-haired girl, quietly spoken and shy. She has a lively four year old daughter, Penny, to whom she is devoted. Jean is also a heroin addict and a single parent. Her life had become chaoatic and there was a chance Penny would be taken into care. Jean lived too far away to come in daily, so we took them both into our hostel, where we have a mother and baby unit. Jean has been able to reduce her methadone intake and Penny attends school. It won't be easy, but the prospects are good and there is every reason to hope that Jean and Penny will become a stable and independent single parent family.

Dr Nathan's policy is not to urge addicts to accept a reduction in their daily medication, but to wait until the suggestion comes from the addict. As the figures of registered drug addicts have risen again, it has become a controversial policy, likened by some to feeding alcoholics with a daily supply of whisky. Kaleidoscope has sad evidence of the dangers of the opposite approach.

Jamie was a pale youth, with dark, curly hair and soft grey eyes. He aroused protective instincts in those who met him and he used his considerable charm to extract from people what he wanted.

Jamie came to the clinic seeking help with a serious drug problem. He said he needed to get away from the squat where he was living with other drug users. His drug habit had already led him into crime and trouble. 'I want some protection,' Jamie said.

Actually, Jamie was already in deep trouble and was due to appear in court. He had decided that it would go well for him in court if he could claim to have overcome his drug addiction while resident at Kaleidoscope. He asked Dr Nathan for a steep reduction in his daily dose of methadone.

Dr Nathan, sensing the weak foundation of Jamie's determination, agreed with reluctance. But when Jamie started to feel the acute physical and psychological pain of withdrawal, he went to another doctor to obtain painkillers. As he further reduced his legal methadone supply, his anxiety increased and he began once again to inject illegal drugs.

One evening he was enjoying a game in the Kaleidoscope reception area before going to bed. Next morning, one of his friends in the hostel found him in a coma. He died later at hospital. A decision to give up drugs can be helped in various ways, but it cannot be forced by courts or concerned parents.

Jamie's death, at the beginning of 1985, was the first to occur at Kaleidoscope since the rebuilding of the premises in 1977, but it was soon to be followed by a second, eerily similar death.

Robert had also been told that he would be rewarded for giving up his drug addiction—he was offered parole from prison. Aged 20, Robert did not come across as odd or remarkable in any way. He had a pretty, bright girlfriend, Deborah, who dressed in Punk style and who had lived with him before he went to prison.

Robert was loaded with good intentions. He promised his probation officer he would not let him down. Deborah said she would leave him if he returned to his drug habit.

'I'll do it,' said Robert. 'Give me £30 today. And I'll give you that same £30 back in a week's time, just to prove that I can resist the temptation to go and buy drugs.'

Having spent months in prison, Robert was technically drug-free, detoxicated. Shirley, Kaleidoscope's nurse, took on the task of maintaining close contact with Robert.

He was at Kaleidoscope for four weeks, pleasant but elusive. A loner, he spent much time away from the community and Shirley eventually put pressure on him to participate. He agreed he would start regular work in the Kaleidoscope bakery.

The morning Robert was due to put on his baker's hat, Shirley found a note. 'Sorry I couldn't make the bakery today. Didn't mean to let you down, but I had an urgent appointment. I'll definitely be there tomorrow. See you. Robert.'

The next day Shirley found his body, overdosed and choked on vomit. There was a note, which read: 'I'm sorry about this, but I couldn't make it. I couldn't tell anyone, but I fixed up with some heroin the day I left prison. I love you, Deborah, but I can't give this up. I'm sorry mum and dad. It's only a matter of time before this catches up with me so I have to take the only way out I know. Sorry to let you down too Shirley. Thanks for everything. Robert.'

Not long after the grim business of contacting Deborah and Robert's parents and arranging for the body to be removed for autopsy, I was on the road to Amersham, fifty miles away, to talk to a meeting organised by Pagoda—Parents against drug abuse; one of many parents' self-help and educational groups which have sprung up around the country.

I was worried about the meeting before I left, since I had been informed the programme involved showing a film 'Better Dead'. I arrived, anxious, sorrowful and stressed in time to hear the opening item—a talk by a pharmacist designed to inform concerned parents about the detailed characteristics of drugs.

As I then watched the lurid film, my anger mounted. It tells of two addicts who renounce their drugs, but spends most of its time in close focus upon needles entering blistered skin and contains a sequence horrific to anyone but a medical professional, where a dead addict's body is deposited for autopsy in its paper shroud by a mechanical grabbing device. The pathologist then calls out the grim evidence of mortal destruction for listing on a white marker board.

Meanwhile, as the audience clutches its stomach in anguish, the reformed addicts are seen boarding a plane for a holiday in Spain. Dressed in the snappiest of clothes, they have made it safely back to the ramparts of the successful.

'I want you to know,' I began, 'that I have watched that film with horror, disgust and anger. Today I have seen the real death of a real addict and the use of material like this and its showing to young people can do nothing but harm.

'Of course if you show it to a class of schoolchildren, it will horrify nearly all of them. It will even make some of them sick. I have heard of cases where this has happened. And it will convince the majority that drug addicts are filthy, stupid and horrible people.

'But these are the kids who would not have taken dangerous drugs anyway. The few who are at risk are those sitting in the back row, who are already alienated and suspicious. They will see these pictures as something fascinating in its ability to shock teachers and anyone else who is presenting the film. And the ending of the film is a lie. Detoxification does not happen like that. As your chairman has already told you, the happy couple at the end of the film are not still in that situation. Both are now dead.'

—'I've had enough of this,' came a voice from the middle of the hall, where about 90 people were sitting. 'It's easy for you to criticise. What are we supposed to do about this problem? Nothing?'

I proceeded to explain the story of Kaleidoscope and its quieter, more patient approach.

—'The point is that you cannot force people to give up drugs. And we cannot simply abandon them. What your group should be doing is campaigning for facilities of the kind we provide at Kaleidoscope in this area.'

A few days later a letter arrived from Pagoda. Thanking me for speaking to the meeting, it continued, 'The film was as controversial as we expected it to be. Some people obviously shared your opinion, but it seemed that the majority held the opposite view.'

The following Friday night, there was a new face at the Kaleidoscope club. A probation officer from Amersham had brought a young addict, in the hope that Kaleidoscope could help.

—'I know your talk didn't go down well with everyone,' the probation officer told me. 'But some of us knew what you were talking about. Phil here has tried, but cannot face the idea of giving up drugs. I cannot find any way in Amersham of providing a maintenance prescription and proper support for him. Can you do anything?' This turned out to be the first of a series of referrals from the Amersham area.

Deborah also had some unfinished business at Kaleidoscope. A couple of days after Robert's death, she arrived to talk to myself and Shirley, accompanied by her sister. Tearful and wretched, the girls sat in the church office and asked me what had happened.

I did my best to explain.

'Is there somewhere we can go to pray,' sobbed Deborah.

Shirley and I went with the two girls into the prayer chapel; a tiny room off the main chapel with little natural light and space for only a handful of people. Both girls instinctively fell to their knees.

'Would you like me to pray with you?' I asked. The girls nodded.

'We thank you God, for your limitless mercy,' I began. 'And we thank you for the love you have shown to Robert. We know that you would feel the goodness of Robert's resolve and of his deep desire to be faithful to his promises.

'We commend Robert to your infinite mercy, Lord. Cleanse him Jesus, from his sin and make him perfect, as he wished to be when he was with us.'

I pronounced the benediction, making the sign of the cross on the foreheads of the no-longer crying girls. The two girls were sorrowful, but also humble. They did not seek to blame, but truly mourned. They knew the strange comfort of God.

'Thank you, Eric,' said Deborah, as they left the chapel and walked down the Kaleidoscope ramp to the streets of Kingston.

7: Branching Out

By the early 1980s, Kaleidoscope's work had settled into a basic pattern, but it still had the power to surprise visitors, who by now arrived in their dozens each week.

'I never imagined it was such a large complex,' is the usual first reaction, when a visitor is shown round. In addition to the main hostel building and the three-storey building which houses the church, community hall, club and medical centre, Kaleidoscope has also expanded into other nearby facilities.

The Magnet education unit, located in a disused public house, has an art workshop, humanities room and an area for scientific work and computers. When this building is demolished for a bypass scheme, it is planned to move the education work to new premises alongside the main Kaleidoscope complex. The church has bought two gracious Victorian houses, which are being restored to accommodate a manse, tutor's accommodation and tutorial rooms. The houses will be joined to the courtyard by an art workshop designed by David Cole, the architect of the original complex. This will bring the work of the church, Kaleidoscope and the education unit onto the same site for the first time.

Down in the basement of the Kaleidoscope, alongside the club, there is also a bakery, where a baker works each day alongside residents to produce bread and other baked goods for sale and for use in the club. The bakery replaced a carpentry workshop, which for two years provided a small unit for unemployed young people in the area.

The idea is constantly to exceed expectations; to resist Kaleidoscope lapsing into the institutional style visitors expect of a day centre or hostel.

'We came here to study drug addiction,' said one shocked visitor, as she watched the crowd of well-dressed, mainly middle-class people settling down to a vegetarian lunch in the Kaleidoscope club. 'What are these people doing here?'

'They are teachers from Tiffin Boys' school across the road,' explains Adele. 'Our aim is as far as we can to involve all sections of the community in our work. In addition to the teachers, we have parents of children who attend the playgroup in the community hall and other visitors.

'In any case, there are only three people at any one time with drug problems resident in the hostel and about three dozen who come each day as outpatients.

'We don't want drug addicts to dominate the atmosphere. The aim is to re-integrate them into the wider community, along with ex-offenders or anyone else who feels alienated.

'Establishing day centres for problem groups often serves only to reaffirm social isolation.'

'But how do you manage to retain this level of enthusiasm and commitment after all these years?'

'We have been going for seventeen years,' I explain, 'and we keep going for many reasons. Practical arrangements, like the fact that all staff have a four-day break after each fortnight of duty. But I don't think that is so important as the inspiration which comes from the daily service of holy communion.'

Kaleidoscope's work is based upon the biblical vision of the Kingdom of God, where everyone and everything is brought into creative harmony. Kaleidoscope is working out the Kingdom of God, which is celebrated in Christian worship.

Our aim from the beginning has been both to preach the

the Kingdom and to be a practical demonstration of that same Kingdom. We want to liberate land, in line with the Old Testament idea of a Promised Land. This is the search for an ideal, but earthly environment.

That is why Kaleidoscope takes such care over its gardens, its art work and its cooking. The red Aga cooker, the copper lamps and the handsome Welsh dresser—a product of the carpentry workshop—are intended as symbols of homecoming. The concept owes something to the story of the prodigal son in the New Testament. However much we rebel, we all in the end need to come home.

But the environment does not strike all visitors as benign. One Monday evening, as Mary and I were walking, two visitors came through the courtyard towards the hostel. One put her fingers into her ears and said, 'I don't know how you stand it!' The party stood still for a moment and sure enough, Indian music was coming from the community hall, where the local Hindu group holds meetings; the church choir was practising Bach in the church and the unmistakable beat of heavy rock music could be felt in the paving tiles from the club beneath. Without out mountain-top retreat in Wales and regular four-day breaks, this would probably have become intolerable.

The administration of the project has become complex and requires the attention of a full-time administrator, George Short, a former teacher, with back-up from professional accountants and lawyers.

By 1985, the project had an annual financial turnover in excess of £150,000. The main items are salaries, £90,000; lighting and heating, £10,000; food, £20,000.

Most of this money comes from local authority sponsorship of those residents 'in care', or entitled to statutory funding of some other type. But an increasing number of residents are not fully funded and the project depends upon grants and donations to meet an annual shortfall of over £30,000. From the earliest days, the Hilden Charitable Fund has contributed about £5,000 a year.

The John Bunyan Church pays the minister's salary and is responsible for appointing the director of the Kaleidoscope project. The ideal situation, in the church's view, is for the same person to hold the office of both minister and director—as is now the case. Several Kaleidoscope staff members are also members of the church. The aim is to keep the links between the church and the project as close as possible.

The church secretary, Alan Roberts, noted in his 1982 annual report to the church meeting, that Kaleidoscope has in some respects outgrown the church. But looking forward from what was then the 100th anniversary of the John Bunyan Baptist Church, he wrote:

'It will be noted that the work of the Kaleidoscope project now forms a large part of this report—a situation entirely appropriate since it forms the major part of the church's activity. Certainly the offspring has outgrown the parent in terms of the resources employed and activities undertaken. We have thus moved away from being a typical Baptist church both in theology and support structure. Nevertheless, our mainspring remains the worship of God and faithful preaching of the Word.

'There are those who would criticise what they believe to be an overemphasis upon the social gospel. However, we are convinced that in serving others we both meet and serve the God we honour and whose name we love. In entering the second century of our church's history we need to remind ourselves of the sublime vision—the

the creation of the Kingdom of God on earth as it is in heaven. We are called to recommit ourselves to securing that vision; nothing more nothing less.'

In all around 400 people are involved in Kaleidoscope in one way or another—either by attending the club, the church, the playgroup or activities such as modern dance and ballet in the community hall.

In addition to drug addicts, the hostel deals with a wide variety of problems and people—sufferers from anorexia nervosa, the slimming disease; unmarried girls expecting babies; ex-offenders and others who for one reason or another cannot survive on their own.

Kaleidoscope is not seen as the church doing something on behalf of the underprivileged. It primarily involves church members and others taking responsibility for their community and being active to control the development of land for the good of the community and to shape the kind of services needed in the area. Respect for the self-determination of others precludes the fixing of political goals, but the aim of the social and academic education within the project is that people will be better equipped to participate effectively and creatively in society.

Jane was one of the first anorectics to live in the hostel. A tall, slim girl, with a naïve, ready laugh, she could be extrovert at a party, but at heart is a very serious young lady. Roman Catholic by upbringing, as a teenager she was drawn to evangelical christianity and took up a leading role in the Christian Union at her College of Further Education.

After two years' treatment at a hospital, Jane's psychiatrist suggested that she should not return home because the anxiety which caused her weight loss had, he felt, much to do with her relationship with her parents. Since Kaleidoscope's hostel looks so pleasant and is run by well-educated people, the psychiatrist's judgment was that Jane would feel at home there.

On her first night, Jane wandered downstairs to the reception area of the hostel, where a member of staff is always on duty to operate the switchboard and provide a social focus for residents.

'When do people normally settle down here?' she asked. It was 9.30 pm. The other residents sniggered.

'Most people go to bed between 11 and midnight,' the staff member told Jane.

'Well how am I supposed to study and pass exams if people stay up half the night making a row?' said the indignant girl.

'Well it's not that unusual,' said Justin, our eldest son, who happened to be home from university. 'At university people don't go to bed all that early.'

Poor Jane had been told by her parents that anyone expecting to succeed academically should be in bed by 9.30 pm. In Jane's mind, this had become a deeply anxious barrier to progress.

The atmosphere in the Kaleidoscope hostel has much in common with a multi-occupied student house. It is noisy, untidy, only just clean and not really very well furnished. This makes it an ideal place for the rehabilitation of anorectics, who are usually over anxious about personal hygiene, tidiness, correctness and every aspect of personal behaviour. They are also often expert at leading their parents a dance.

Lisa was particularly skilled in this art and succeeded in spinning an unbreakable web of worry around her parents. Kaleidoscope staff decided that if Lisa was to grow up, it was necessary for her parents to contact her only once a month by appointment.

The parents arrived for the first visit in unforgettable style. Lisa's father was dressed in black and wore a large crucifix. As he shook my hand heartily, he revealed that he was a lay reader.

Lisa's mother was a larger, maternal lady with a smock and pink skin. She was nursing a black baby, who appeared to be having difficulty with breathing. Lisa's mother smiled brightly and said, 'This is the 23rd child I've fostered. This poor little thing has quite severe asthma. I tend to take the ones no one else wants.'

It was immediately obvious why Lisa wished to remain little and helpless and a problem. Her mother needed her to be like that. Lisa's father then asked if he could lead in prayer. He prayed that God would bless Lisa, keep her on the narrow path and use her to God's greater glory. Serious conversation then began.

'Well, how are you getting on, Lisa? How is she getting on, Mr Blakebrough?' Before I could speak, Lisa began.

'I've been doing alright,' she said, 'but I'm not quite feeling myself today . . . Something happened yesterday.'

'What?' enquired the anxious parents.

'I spent the night in hospital. I took an overdose.'

'An overdoes? What of? Why?'

'Paracetemol. It was nothing really, just a silly thing. I'm quite alright.'

So far Lisa had been telling no more than the truth, although her timing and her manner had an air of dramatic intent about it. As her parents relaxed at her explanation, they enquired about her violin playing.

'I don't play any more,' she said.

'And why not?' asked her father.

'I no longer have my violin.'

'Why? What happened to it?'

'Well, I didn't really want to tell you, but . . . I sold it.'

'Sold it? For goodness sake why did you do that, you weren't in need of money were you?'

'I'm afraid I was. You see there's something else I haven't told you. I have another problem. Now you mustn't worry, but I've been taking something worse than paracetemol. Heroin.'

At this the parents were in tears of alarm. How long had she been doing this? Why hadn't she told them? Was it this place? And how had she financed such a thing?

At this final question, Lisa cast her eyes to the ground and whispered. 'There are ways,' she snuffled. 'There are ways a girl who is desperate can always earn a little money.'

Beyond the paracetemol drama, which was itself related to the fact that the parental visit was due, the entire story was untrue, although it required urine and blood tests to prove that she was deceiving her parents.

Lisa lived two years in the hostel and coped. But eventually she persuaded her parents to take her away. Three years later, she was still under the care of a psychiatrist.

Lisa was a particularly difficult case. Other anorectics have proved well suited, after initial difficulties, to Kaleidoscope's informal educational methods and most have obtained the necessary qualifications to go on to university or college.

Subjects offered at any time depend upon the skills and qualifications of staff. Several of the staff have teaching qualifications and Kaleidoscope has a full-time artist, so it has been possible to offer a fairly broad range of humanities subjects, including three languages. There is also tuition in electronics, general science and a range of general classes, also open to other people in the community, on politics, economics and current affairs.

Genevieve was one girl who clearly benefitted from the

education unit. When she first arrived at Kaleidoscope for interview, she seemed an unpromising referral. She had been a drug addict for more than ten years and there seemed little hope of making real progress with her.

Genevieve's social worker pointed out that the girl had a very high IQ—over 140. Further inquiry revealed that she also had professional parents and a thoroughly middle-class background. Although she had truanted from school since the age of 13, she had read very widely.

'What you need, Genevieve is a degree,' I pronounced.

Genevieve, who had expected to hear about detoxification regimes, targets and discipline looked interested. The next day she was in the hostel and nine months later she passed two GCE A-levels. Unfortunately, Genevieve then inherited a large sum of money, bought a cottage in the country and lost her sense of purpose. When last heard of, she was in the care of a probation officer in another part of the country.

Achieving a balance of young people in the hostel has proved essential. During one period, an entire flat of six bedrooms was occupied by 16-year-old girls who had been brought up in children's homes. The dominant girl organised the others in a shop-lifting squad, which was only stopped when two of the girls were evicted from the hostel.

Kaleidoscope has also had to discover its limitations. Problems of chronic mental illness are uncontainable, as staff realised when they agreed to John Frazer, a social worker, having assured them that his history in psychiatric hospitals could be broken in the right environment. By the third night of his residence, John was banging his head violently against his wall. When staff went to investigate, he locked himself in the bathroom and wedged himself behind the toilet, from where it took hours to remove him. The psychiatrist said it was attention-seeking, which had to be tolerated and lived through.

Three days later, after numerous other incidents of bogus fire alarms and other disturbances, John challenged a member of staff to fight and produced a dagger. When that incident was defused, he smuggled a box into a staff room labelled 'HMG—explosives'.

'There's a time fuse on that. I'll blow the lot of you to pieces,' he said. The police were called, cordoned off the area, and crawled into the room and found a box full of fishing tackle.

Although there were good moments, even with such a violent and unpredictable person—John appeared at an Ebenezer supper in the community hall and gave a thrilling rendering of a song he had written about the deceptions of propaganda—eventually he became insupportable. A physical assault on a staff member led to his return to mental hospital.

The task of selecting residents from the large number of referrals made to the hostel used to be done by the whole staff team at their weekly meeting. Now it is trusted to Mary and Adele, because continuity and experience are of such importance. Dr Nathan is consulted when there is a question of mental health.

The aim is balance; a community where harmonious relationships can be established. The construction of a corner of the Kingdom of God on earth.

8: Street Level

On Friday nights at around 10 pm, the hostel population empties out into the Kaleidoscope club.

Friday night club, from 10.00 pm to 6 am, is Kaleidoscope's longest running institution. It has survived three changes of building, but its purpose today is little changed from the first occasion when Jan and her friends decided to keep the club open all night, offering nothing more than a pleasant atmosphere, food and drink and an opportunity to be there.

The club is the project's meeting point with the street. It has its own, street-level entrance and is open to anyone. The only rules are those which forbid physical violence and criminal activity.

Just as in the hostel, it is policy to mix different kinds of people in a search for a balanced community, so the club brings together all sorts. The church's goal, counter to the instinct of the many religious people who prefer to separate themselves from evil-doers, is to live alongside those who have deviated from normal social patterns, just as Jesus did. The key to the approach in social terms is that most so-called 'bad behaviour' and 'problems' are in reality symptoms of a person's inability to cope with their life. Kaleidoscope seeks to provide a good situation, good company and a break from an individual's everyday stresses and difficulties.

Kaleidoscope is thus at one with the street agencies working in the field of drug addiction and homelessness, who believe that people suffer because of evil in society—original sin in Biblical terms. This does not mean that individuals are not important, but it does mean that Kaleidoscope works with people in a community setting rather than individually.

Because of the antagonism some young people feel towards orthodox medical services, Kaleidoscope runs its medical service in conjunction with the club, at the same hours. On Friday nights, people who are new to the club find it strange to see the door marked 'Surgery' next to the Ladies and Gents. Like a university, or the armed forces, Kaleidoscope aims to have its services and its values woven into the fabric of its life. Friday night is a mixture of music, food, conversation, hilarity and social service.

Of the hundreds of young people who have spent nights in the Kaleidoscope club, none is more remarkable than Becky, whose life has been lived out in regular contact with Kaleidoscope, chiefly through the club but also briefly when she lived in the original hostel in Cromwell Road.

It is easy to understand the distress deep in the mind of Becky. At the age of four, her father and mother divorced. Her father married again and started a new family. Her mother married again and started a new family. She stayed at first with her mother, but found that she was in love with her father, so she switched houses.

Becky hated her step-mother and once again found herself switching allegiances, returning to her mother. There she was jealous of her mother's new baby and again went back to her father. Finally, she discovered for herself the strong force of sex and left home to stay with a youth four years older than herself. She found she had power over the youth and set out to conquer older and more experienced men.

By her middle teens, Becky had the experience of a worldly

forty-year-old; which is to say that she had experienced the disillusionment and pain normally known by much older people. If a traumatised middle-aged woman sometimes needs to reach for a tranquilliser, Becky needed something a good deal stronger.

Although Becky at different times used and abused every drug that was available on the streets, she was far from being a physical wreck. Indeed, she had both beauty and style. Although capable of extremes and wild shifts of mood and behaviour, she also had a constant side to her—reflected in her relationship with Noel, a short man with a wry sense of humour, who was also deeply involved in the street scene and who always seemed content to act as a fixed star in Becky's rapidly shifting universe.

Becky knew generations of Kaleidoscope staff. She used its medical service , its community and, when she got into trouble with the law, its support. So when, early in 1972 she became pregnant, it was natural that she should move into the hostel during the pregnancy and that the child, Jesse Leon, should become as much a part of Kaleidoscope as Becky herself

The baby was born on July 8th and became a regular at the Friday night club, where he was seen by the club's physician, at the time a young South African, Dr John Wright. Jesse's birth was celebrated with music and candles in the club one Friday night.

Jesse Leon saw some strange things. Like the night that two boys in the club were gambling in a desultory sort of fashion and Stan accused Joe of cheating.

'That fiver belongs to me. You're a cheat,' said Stan.

'Oh come off it,' said Joe. 'It's all in your head.'

As Stan reached for the disputed banknote, Joe siezed his chance. He picked up the five pound note and ate it. It was difficult to deal with a man like Joe. He also set fire to his hair one night. On another occasion he kidnapped the Kaleidoscope rabbit, Frodo, much to Jan's anguish.

But Jesse Leon did not live long enough to understand any of this. On November 8th, 1972, at the age of four months, Becky found him dead in his cot. It was Becky's worst moment. She had hardly been a conventional mother, but Dr Wright knew that she had, with Noel's help, been a good one. He also knew that Jesse had died from that mysterious illness which claims hundreds of babies each year in similar circumstances.

There was a depressing, curt service at the local crematorium. The duty minister did his job, but Becky looked lost. Her friends were not there; her community was missing.

Later that same week, on the Friday night at midnight, the lights of the club were turned up and the music down. I addressed the packed club.

'Most of us know,' I said, 'that Becky's baby, Jesse Leon, has died. Jesse Leon was part of Kaleidoscope. You all knew him. We have to make this a celebration. Can we sit in a circle?' Becky led the way and sat down beside me.

Dr Wright then spoke, explaining the nature of the mysterious respiratory disease which had killed Jesse. He also spoke of Jesse's health record and Becky's excellence as a mother.

Into the silence which followed, another club member spoke.

'I'd like to say something about Noel, too,' he said. 'Most of us know that Jesse wasn't Noel's son. But Noel has supported Becky just as if he was. He's been a real father to Jesse. I admire him for the loyalty he's shown to Becky and the love and care he gave to Jesse.'

'I just want to say how we're all going to miss Jesse,' said a girl. 'It was really good to have him around on Fridays. He was good. Really good.'

I don't think we should be too sad, though,' came the next voice. 'Jesse's gone to a good place. Nirvana. The state of bliss. Nirvana.'

'He was pure and still is pure,' said someone else.

As the voices shifted, expressing support, ideas, visions, I prepared to speak.

'My view is not so different. From my faith, I know that Becky should feel at peace. It is inconceivable that God in his love would not receive a child into his everlasting kingdom.'

At that point, candles were handed around and as the faces bowed over the flames, the anthem of a generation, or this fragment of a generation, was coaxed into the air. 'May the long time sun shine upon you,' they sang. 'May the pure light within you guide you all the way on.'

Finally, I made the sign of the cross on Becky's forehead and, without any awkwardness, the club returned to its merriment and noise. Becky was ready to continue.

9: The Hand of Friendship

Shortly after the death of Jesse Leon, at a time when the Kaleidoscope club was self-evidently dispensing a healing warmth into the community, the club acquired some new regulars.

Late one Friday, ten men walked into the club. They were in their twenties and although two of them were blonde, it seemed that their shoulder-length hair and beards were mainly black. They wore leather or dark denim and all wore denim jerkins with the emblem of a rat embroidered on the back. 'Road Rats, London,' was their identifying message.

They had not been long in the club before a fight broke out. No one could tell how it started, but the ferocity of the fighting was beyond anything previously imaginable.

The telephone was ripped from the wall and smashed. Plates, bottles, mugs—everything breakable—was broken. At one point, a great hexagonal table, eight feet across, was upturned and was being used as a kind of crusher to extinguish the life of a man beneath.

David, myself and a new member of staff, Mike, rushed towards the unconscious man. One of the rats jumped on my back. Mary beat upon the attacker's back with her tiny fists. Blood was streaming from noses and head wounds. Victims were groaning on the floor. The sound of blows from heavy objects thudded. Women screamed. Men punched or kicked writhing bodies. It was difficult to tell who was fighting whom.

At length, the intruders decided their work was complete. They moved out of the club, kicking bodies as they left and glowering their pure bitterness. Their motorcycles were kicked back to life and they were gone.

Mike was the only member of staff badly hurt, but all were shaken. Mary was sobbing. Ambulances and the police were called. From that point, Friday nights were no longer the fulfilment of a dream; they were an eight-hour nightmare.

Their reign of terror lasted around five years. Although they were not always present and when they came they were frequently peaceful, they cast an evil shadow over the club. Everyone was afraid of them. Everyone was meant to be afraid of them.

But gradually, links were formed, respect established. There was no one moment when this breakthrough came, but many incidents which led to understanding.

From the point of view of Kaleidoscope staff, the Road Rats' values gradually became visible. Although capable of horrifying violence, they were not mindless thugs. Their hand-built motorcycles, often lavishly and carefully embellished were evidence of their creativity. They had families and marriages with a strong record of loyalty. Their 'runs', which the public sensed to be bestial forays, were often family outings. They had a strong sense of fun and when, one Christmas, I invited them to the annual church pantomime, they arrived in force, with their children and in a great spirit of merriment.

They also had unmistakable courage. One night I saw them in the car park, preparing for the arrival of another gang which had challenged them to fight. None of them admitted nervousness, but the signs were obvious. But there was no question of stepping back from the challenge.

One night in the club, one of the rats challenged another youth to fight. 'Come on, put up your hands. Defend yourself,' said the Road Rat. I intervened. 'Now be fair,' I said, 'this lad is smaller than you and weaker than you. He's no match for you. Would you accept a challenge to fight someone you knew would beat you?'

The rat spat at me. 'If I didn't know you I'd smash you for that,' he said. 'I'll take on anyone, whatever the odds.' He meant it and I, in accusing him of cowardice, had challenged the group's most sacred tenet.

On another occasion, when I called for order in the club, one of the rats faced up to me and said, 'I suppose you're not frightened. You think God will defend you.'

'No,' I said. 'I don't believe that. I am frightened.' And the tension subsided.

For their part, the rats also began to see both that Kaleidoscope offered a useful service—it was the only all-night facility in Kingston. And on occasions, it provided support in a form the proud rats were prepared to accept.

On a few occasions, the surgery was useful to the rats. One of them turned up early one morning with a serious knife wound in his arm. Seeing that it was partly stitched, the Kaleidoscope nurse asked the man why he had not been properly attended to.

'I went to the casualty,' he said, 'and this wog doctor starts squeezing me here and saying "does this hurt?" and there, "does this hurt?". So I poked him one and said "does this hurt?"'

Another time, one of the rats had badly hurt his eye in a fight. The Kaleidoscope doctor said the man could lose his sight if he did not go to hospital.

'I'm not going up there. Just do your best for me,' said the man.

Hearing the story, I spoke to one of the gang leaders and explained the importance of the hospital attention. Eventually, Andrew Mawson, the assistant minister, took the man by car to Kingston Hospital. The rats seemed to respect people who were prepared to help without needing to be curious about their affairs; who accepted them on their own terms. What they could not stand was anyone attempting to push them around. The wellspring of their aggression seemed so often to be a sense that merely because at school they had been difficult, inarticulate and unsuccessful, they had been punished. Few of them had escaped expulsion and detention centre. The logic of their anger found understanding at Kaleidoscope, even if their expression of it could not. In the end, the rats even seemed to respect the club's guidelines: no violence, no drug dealing.

As time went on, Andrew and I found ourselves called upon to visit members of the group in prison. We got to know wives and families. We sensed strengths and weakness. And we shared good humour.

When I arrived at the prison cell, the guard would invariably express surprise that a 'Hell's Angel', as they were normally wrongly known, was receiving a visit from a parson.

'Well, you didn't know I went to the church youth club every Friday night, did you?' they would joke.

The rats also shared a sense of occasion, almost religious when they were faced with tragedy or something momentous. Thus it was in August 1979 when Becky, at the age of 21, took an overdose of drugs and died. She had got to know the Road Rats and they knew and respected her for her ability to face danger; to live on the edge.

I knew nothing of Becky's death when, one day, a cavalcade of motorcycles arrived at the Kaleidoscope gate. 'Come with us,' they said, explaining what had happened to Becky.

The sight of a minister's car proceeding through London,

with Road Rat outriders, to attend a funeral appeared both shocking and frightening to some of those present at the burial, but the rats were there for a purpose. They did not wish to take part in any Christian ceremony, but they wanted to pay their respect.

That meant leaving their bikes at the cemetery gate and walking to the graveside. There one of the gang threw a single red rose on to the grave. Then they left.

'Becky had to go that way. She lived hard.' Sweep, one of the rats later told me.

The rats themselves certainly courted danger and early in 1984 the whole country got to know about them. The event was a party in Surrey, where the Road Rats had run into another motorcycle group from Devon, known as Satan's Slaves. A fight of awful proportions broke out.

Ossie and Cowboy, two of the rats by now best known to Kaleidoscope, were stabbed to death. Another's stomach was ripped open. A fourth was badly hurt. Two other rats, although not seriously injured, had been shot; one in the hand and one in the back. Many others were in custody and when the press learned of the story, the headlines wrote themselves. There were stories of sexual horror, including one scene in which a girl had been stripped naked, staked to the ground and assaulted.

I heard the news from Cowboy's wife. I could not interest myself in the detail of the horror. Sexual perversion, I reasoned, was not confined to any group within society. I knew the terror the rats could visit upon their foes, but that did not alter the fact that the dead men's wives would feel the deaths as any other woman would feel the death of her man.

I had known Ossie since the time he got his first job at a local ironmongers. It was at the time the original club was being converted to its all-night sessions and I had gone to the shop for some materials. Recognising me, Ossie had refused payment and I had been forced to pay the manger.

Ossie was a handsome, dashing man with black hair, flashing eyes and dazzling smile. Of unpredictable temper, he had once in a moment of anger pointed his motorbike straight into the path of oncoming traffic. Ossie was a daredevil and a ferocious fighter.

Cowboy came from the Midlands. He was a family man who worked hard at a scrap yard and came home tired at night. Most of his money he spent on his home and he was devoted to his family. He went out with the rats most Fridays and regularly turned up at Kaleidoscope in the early hours of a Saturday morning. He was the comedian of the group, especially after he had been drinking.

On the Friday following the fateful party, the club was tense. A few of the rats who were not in custody came to the club with their women. They were shocked and angry at the death of their friends and at the fact that Satan's Slaves had surprised them by being armed with guns. They did not attempt to explain to anyone outside the group exactly what had taken place.

Moll, a close friend of Ossie, asked me to conduct the funeral of the dead men. Later, the parents of Ossie requested Father John Cremin, the local Roman Catholic priest, to conduct their son's service. I agreed to attend the funeral of Ossie and to conduct the service for Cowboy.

The arrangements were elaborate. Hundreds of Hell's Angels and affiliated groups were due to attend and the police agreed to co-operate with the plan for a funeral procession of motorbikes behind the cortege. A lorry was included to carry the floral tributes, many of them in the shape of rats or other emblems of the fraternity.

The funeral services followed usual patterns. Both churches were packed and there was much weeping. In my address, I made no reference to the charges made against the Road Rats. I knew, as they all did, some of the evil which had been done, but knew also the good side of their comradeship. I spoke of the depth of their commitment to each other, of their sense of fun and their courage. Prayers were said for God's mercy and forgiveness and for his blessing upon those who mourned.

After the coffin was lowered into the ground, each member of the Road Rats took a turn at filling in the grave.

The filling in of graves took two or three hours, during which time the grim-looking crowd of mourners stood in small groups or singly. Spaced apart, they appeared to fill the whole cemetry. They looked like some forlorn army burying its dead. Andrew, Adele and myself, dressed in green and white cassocks, moved among them, clasping hands, exchanging a greeting or expressing some words of understanding. There was a real bond.

A few days after the funeral, I went to the prison to visit those in custody. It was a sad occasion. A mixture of grief, shock, anger and anxiety.

Almost a year later, the trial took place at Winchester Crown Court. A large part of one wall of the court room was given over to a display of weapons—pick handles, spades, forks, knives, guns, tent pegs and mallets. The evidence plainly put the Road Rats in the worst light and the Satan's Slaves pleaded that they had acted in self-defence.

The prosecution of the trial and the press coverage, gave the impression that the Road Rats went hunting every weekend for women to abuse and rape and for groups of young men to wound or kill.

To me, this was a grotesque caricature, designed to evoke sentences longer than justice demanded. I offered to speak on Muff's behalf, since Muff was being presented as the most monstrous member of a depraved group.

'I can tell you about these men because I know them,' I told the court. 'I have known them for more than ten years.

'In that time, it is true that when I first knew them they were a terror to our neighbourhood. But that was a long time ago. Since then, I have seen them most weeks in the club my church runs each Friday and they have been generally law abiding. I also know that these men are all deeply shocked at the death of their two colleagues. Perhaps this could be taken into account in assessing a sentence.

'As for Muff here. I have to say that in this group, which I have watched frequently, Muff is a leader, but at the Kaleidoscope club I have on two or three occasions seen him use that leadership to stop fights. I find the picture presented by the prosecution impossible to square with the individual I know.

'It is also wrong to believe that the Road Rats are marauding barbarians. Most of their activities are those typical of a motorcycle club. They involve a group of bikers riding together and causing no trouble to the general public. The Road Rats went to this house expecting a good party. It got out of hand and the consequences were fatal.

'If the court could be as lenient as possible, perhaps the Road Rats and Satan's Slaves could be reconciled.'

The judge was clearly not impressed. He said that Muff's evidence was full of 'nauseating hypocrisy' and sentenced him to eight years' imprisonment. One, for a first offence, received five years.

The club was subdued after the trial, but the Rats have continued to arrive at Kaleidoscope. Since the trial, they have gained new members. But the main change in the club has been the marked increase again in the number of drug addicts.

Ron the tramp, who has spent much of his life sitting in the reception of the Kaleidoscope hostel in recent years, still comes to the club and manages to sleep laying full length on a thin bench, heedless of the noise. Noel, perhaps the first person to cross the threshold of the old Kaleidoscope Club in 1968, still comes most Fridays. Every day, some ex-resident or ex-club member drops in to talk.

On the Friday night before Christmas, there is a tradition of giving mince pies to everyone who is in the club at midnight. Residents, ex-residents and others who are homeless will meet again for lunch on Christmas Day, but for the club, the Friday night before Christmas is the last club night of the old year.

As I distributed the pies at Christmas, 1984, I offered one to a tall stranger, dressed in black leather. He was not wearing the colours which distinguish different motorbike groups, but I guessed he might be one of the Road Rats I had not met.

'Happy Christmas,' I said, holding out the plate.

The stranger took the pie and said, 'This is my first visit to the club. I came here to thank you for what you said on behalf of Muff. You were the only person who had a good word to say for any of us.

'I know the judge didn't thank you for what you said, but I want to thank you. This is a great place and you're doing a great job. Thanks.'

He then gave me a special handshake, which I recognised as a sign of their fraternity.

Humbled at the tribute, I crept behind the Welsh dresser to hide my embarrassment and felt grateful to God. The next Sunday, in my sermon, I recounted the incident to the church.

'That symbol of our relationship with this group of people. That tribute and that gratitude is made to all of us who have given ourselves to this work. It is made to this church. We should thank God.'

10: Kissing God

'Kissing God', a play by Phil Young, was commissioned by the BBC and the Hampstead Theatre. The author researched his play at Kaleidoscope and several other projects dealing with drug addiction in the United Kingdom.

Although not based directly on people at Kaleidoscope, the characters in the play are clearly recognisable to the staff of the project. Act I introduces Amy, and Mark her landlord. She is attractive, a ballet dancer, happy in her new flat. Her landlord is rather dull, but obliging. It comes as a shock to discover that Amy is addicted to heroin and that Mark is her source of supply.

Act II takes place a year later. Amy's addiction has extracted its price, the flat is bare, the few remaining items of clothing are strewn about the place. Mark is involved with her in a love – hate relationship, and his addiction is now totally out of control.

The two other characters in the play are Babbli and Harry. Babbli is a resident at a hostel which caters for homeless young people in need of care and Harry is a resident in a rehabilitation hostel for drug addicts. Both pretend to have flats of their own, and both are anxious the other does not discover the truth.

Unlike many educational films on the subject of drug abuse, this play is not propaganda. It carefully exposes the insecurities which we all experience. Amy is guilty about having had a late abortion. Mark has sexual problems. Babbli is ashamed of being illegitimate. Harry is too sophisticated to reveal his problems, but in one eloquent moment he declares with emotion that he is afraid.

Babbli, like most of the residents in the Kaleidoscope hostel, is not a drug addict. She inhabits the twilight world of the homeless and rootless simply because she has no close relationship with her parents and as yet has no place to call her own. But she is cheerful and brave, and it seems likely that she will choose a good way in life and overcome her difficulties. Babbli deals with her problems partly by working hard. It seems that she is aware of this because at one point in the play she declares 'we are all addicted to something'.

This is the first truth about addiction: we are all addicted to something. There is a great void in our being, our mortality alone ensures that this is so. Many executives who have been made redundant have experienced this feeling of emptiness. Those who have been bereaved, and those who have been divorced, know the almost intolerable pain of aloneness. We all deal with this aloneness in different ways, and it is not surprising that in this age of wonder drugs, some young people have turned to drugs for relief from their insecurity.

Everyone experiences anger. Life is unfair and there are good reasons to feel anger. Some people have been treated outrageously and hurt very deeply. One expression of anger is refusing to eat. A baby in a tantrum throws its food away.

Suicide is often an expression of anger. But suicide is too final. A person who kills himself cannot witness the distress he causes. Drug addiction can be a form of slow suicide, causing pain to people who are meant to care and alarm to others who are complacent.

Drug addiction is probably always caused by deep insecurity, or feelings of anger, but the drug scene also has a certain attraction. Since a period between childhood and maturity has been recognised, teenagers have coveted their own secret societies. An eleven year old girl will laugh at her mother's idea of suitable clothes or shoes. Pop music creates an opportunity for participation in dancing according to the latest style. To call a group a band, or a band a group, shows that a person is completely out of touch.

One fashion among a sizable section of young people is drug taking. The practice is not by any means new, but it has replaced getting drunk among some groups of young people. Like alcohol, regular abuse can lead to serious problems for many individuals. In every big centre of population a few young people die every year from an overdose of drugs.

The attraction of becoming a drug addict is easy to understand. It is the ultimate in abuse. People may not admire an addict, but at least they recognise the addict for something. Degeneracy has always had a certain notoriety, and notoriety is akin to fame.

Fashion and availability together determine which drugs are abused. In the early 1960s cannabis, LSD and heroin were popular. In the 1970s barbiturates were widely abused, then amphetamines. The drugs scene varies somewhat from locality to locality. At Kaleidoscope, there was a short period when alcohol seemed to take over from drugs, and another time when pseudo-homosexual activities became the style. The early 1980s was the era of Polyabuse—abusing anything and everything. Solvent abuse became fashionable particularly among skinheads. In 1984, heroin again became the main drug of abuse, although other drugs are still used among a minority.

Cannabis is still widely abused, but is easily detected because of its distinctive smell. Drug traffickers, however, faced no such problem in importing pharmaceutical products destined for the black market. Recently international crime syndicates have exploited political instability in a number of opium-growing countries to steeply increase sales to a group of customers whose loyalty is guaranteed because heroin is particularly addictive.

Another factor which causes a drug to lose popularity is unwanted side effects. LSD is often tried, but usually given up after bad 'trips'—a bad trip being a prolonged waking nightmare, sometimes triggering serious psychotic illness. Barbiturates caused many addicts to become violent, and their speech and gait were affected. This gave barbiturates a bad image and many abusers rejected them as first choice, although they are still a second choice when heroin is difficult to obtain.

There are predictions that cocaine will follow heroin as the most popular drug to abuse. This is based on the over-production of cocaine in several debt-laden Latin American countries and therefore the likelihood that traffickers will try to market the surplus in Europe. Also, the 1985 government campaign to stop drug abuse focused especially upon the dangers of heroin. This may give heroin a bad image and cause abusers to switch to cocaine.

Previously cocaine has been very expensive and used mainly by the jet set. Devotees of cocaine have claimed that it is less addictive than heroin, but there is plenty of evidence that it can become a habit and cause serious damage to health.

Solvent abuse became popular among small groups, or gangs. Some individuals become seriously addicted, and in a very few cases this can cause damage to a person's mental health. Most groups, however, stop abusing solvents within a year or two of starting. Some fatalities have occurred from the use of aerosols and from suffocation when a plastic bag has been put over the head, and there are reports of a few fatal accidents to people intoxicated by solvents.

In considering measures for the prevention and treatment of drug abuse, it is important to keep in mind some of the causes. The underlying psychological causes must not be overemphasised. We are all addicted to something. We all suffer insecurity and anger.

Drug abuse is not a disease to be treated by the medical profession. In a small number of cases, mental illness may be diagnosed, and abuse can sometimes trigger a serious psychotic illness. Psychiatric treatment is not, however, appropriate in most cases.

Relatives and friends of addicts speak of their changed personality, their moral degeneracy and social malfunctioning. This is not primarily caused by drugs. The craving for drugs leads to crime and vice in those people who cannot finance a growing habit from a legitimate income. Lying and pleading become a means of survival.

The personality changes associated with drug abuse seem to confirm popular opinion that drug addicts are psychopaths. This misconception reinforces the practice in the United Kingdom of treating drug addicts in psychiatric departments of hospitals.

Psychiatrists have been among the first to recognise that hospital treatment is not appropriate in most cases of drug addiction. The trend has therefore been towards a short period in hospital to achieve detoxification, followed by a period of about two years of residence at a rehabilitation hostel.

Rehabilitation hostels have developed a variety of programmes, but most are based upon the assumption that addicts need to completely rebuild their lives, recognising that they need the strict discipline imposed by a hierarchy among the residents of the hostel. This hierarchy is formed from those residents who have developed a degree of responsibility.

Each rehabilitation hostel has its own emphasis. Some believe in daily group therapy, some believe that personal conversion to Christ is the only answer. The aim is the same; to bring about a complete change in the life of the addict.

It is not difficult to understand why most addicts are not prepared to undergo detoxification followed by rehabilitation. Apart from the fact that an addict needs to give an absolute priority to obtaining up to £20 a day for drugs and therefore has not enough time for hospital appointments, an addict is scared of being withdrawn from drugs.

Kaleidoscope's emphasis is different to that of other treatment centres. The attempt is made to reverse the process of addiction. Initially a medically prescribed drug is given. When there is no longer the need for lying, dealing and stealing in order to buy drugs, a person can begin to revert to normal patterns of behaviour. The prescribed dose can be gradually reduced, and in many cases complete withdrawal is accomplished over a period of time.

Critics of maintenance prescribing claim that it merely substitutes a legal drug for an illegal one, that addicts sell part of their prescriptions, and that many people given maintenance prescriptions never come off drugs, but remain in a state of addiction.

It is true that where addicts are given a week's supply of drugs they are likely to sell part of their prescription. For this reason Kaleidoscope prescribes methadone in liquid form which has to be swallowed in front of a member of the staff. The addict must come each day to the centre which establishes a daily routine.

Giving an addict a daily dose of methadone will not in itself encourage a person to request gradual withdrawal. However the tedium and time absorbed in having to go to receive medication each day is a disincentive to continue the habit. A positive incentive is created by offering the addict the prospect of an improvement in his lifestyle if he can become drug free. This is achieved by the personal concern of the staff, educational and training facilities in addition to an encouragement to join the social activities open to the rest of the community which enrich a person's social life. Critics of our methods who have not visited Kaleidoscope often say: 'Just giving people methadone has proved over and over again to be ineffectual in bringing about any significant change in the addict.' We agree that *just* giving someone methadone will not work. Kaleidoscope, however, offers a rich social environment, unlike many of the hospital drug dependency units which followed a methadone maintenance policy. Kaleidoscope's priorities are well illustrated by its staffing ratio, which provides three medical professionals and 15 non-medical staff.

We do not believe that the first task is to take the addict off drugs. Making that the first requirement is like asking a non-swimmer to jump in at the deep end. It is a frightening prospect.

We begin by prescribing methadone in quantities roughly equivalent to those the addict has been used to in the form of heroin. In this way the addict is relieved of the panic of being required to give up drugs quickly or painfully.

Another reason for this procedure is the recognition that much of the antisocial behaviour of addicts is not due to a psychopathic condition. It is due to the lying, stealing and vice which have often become a necessary way of life in order to buy drugs. Harsh discipline and an authoritarian regime can cause behaviour modification, but the danger is that the ex-addict acquires a new identity of superior strength acquired by discipline. This is an unpleasant notion and often damaging to the person concerned.

There are a number of people who have gone through rehabilitation hostels who continue to identify themselves as ex-addicts. These people wish to work with other addicts. They constantly attend meetings about drug abuse and they still seem obsessed by the subject. They have hardly been liberated and they go about their daily life with an inner feeling that they are in some way vulnerable to an illness.

This is a thoroughly unhelpful view. The truth is that everyone is vulnerable to addiction because we are all to some extent angry and insecure.

I have often been distressed when I have visited a so-called therapy group in prison, or a similar institution, where addicts are engaged in group work. The message is reinforced frequently that they are psychopaths, that they are a total mess, that they are unworthy of respect. Such abject sentiments are unnecessary. The simple truth is that in trying to deal with insecurity and anger they turn to drugs. Eventually the habit became an obsession because every day they had to worry about them. This often led to actions which an individual would not normally have contemplated.

This is not a symptom of grave psychological illness. It is simply a fact that if your body craves drugs you will do almost anything to stop the craving. Why exaggerate the problem by blaming it on some mythical illness? Kaleidoscope rejects this disease concept. We try to reverse the process of addiction.

A comprehensive approach which aims at improving social life, is not only a valuable aid to recovery from addiction, it is also an important preventative measure in the case of young people who are experiencing unhappiness in many areas of their lives. Most drug abuse does not lead on to addiction. A happy social life is the best antidote. This simple observation is overlooked in many of the more intensive programmes for the prevention and treatment of drug abuse.

Kaleidoscope is concerned with the whole of its local community. The project caters for a great variety of people, only a small proportion of whom are involved in any form of drug abuse.

Among those who abuse drugs, only a minority are truly addicted. Many who have problems associated with drug taking are not addicts. Kaleidoscope helps many with drug problems by means of counselling and the provision of recreational activities. Methadone maintenance is only prescribed for chronic addicts.

Some facts and figures relating to methadone maintenance at Kaleidoscope may be helpful. In a recent sample of 32 chronic addicts we found that:

— six had moved out of our area and were referred to other agencies;
— seven dropped out and two had to be suspended because they were found to be using other drugs in addition to methadone;
— six were entirely successful in coming off drugs and have been drug-free for more than 12 months;
— seven were more stable and continued on maintenance;
— two went to prison for crimes committed before treatment began;
— two died.

It can be seen from these figures that in effect, out of this group of 17 who stayed in the programme, one third were rated as complete successes and about the same number were stable. Those who continue to receive maintenance are not failures. Methadone maintenance does not cure heroin addiction, but properly used this method of treatment can enable addicts to live an almost normal life. If the addict then becomes involved in creative activities and ceases to be over-anxious about drugs, there is the possibility of complete withdrawal at a later date.

Deaths caused by an overdose of drugs are not always accidental. Many deaths are suicides. One psychiatrist who treats drug addicts states that those addicts whose parents support them do not die, but those addicts whose parents reject them do die. That is certainly not true. Many loving and supportive parents have lost a son or daughter as a result of a drug overdose, and some addicts give their parents no option but to ask them to leave home. It is true, however, that addicts need to be loved while they are still addicts. Love is unconditional. This rule applies to all who seek to serve others: genuine care must always be unconditional. Caring with a view to reforming people, curing them or converting them is always wrong.

About a third of young people who abuse drugs briefly, or intermittently over a period of a few years, will cease using without any form of treatment. It is possible to identify many of those who are most at risk. A placement in a hostel, such as the one at Kaleidoscope, will often prevent a vulnerable person becoming dependent on drugs.

This success rate does not compare well with the claims made by some other agencies. Phoenix House, for example, a leading rehabilitation hostel, has recently started to claim a more than 90 per cent success for those who can stay its extremely rigorous course. But such figures have to be set against the fact that in Kaleidoscope's experience less than one in a hundred addicts will voluntarily accept a Phoenix House type regime.

It is often questioned if catering for a wide variety of young people does not cause the spread of drug abuse. Unless special isolation units are established it is inevitable that such mixing will occur within the community.

It is not possible to keep people from temptation. It is the rejection of certain people by the community which aggravates problems and may lead to more serious drug abuse. Providing there is a good social environment, contact with drug addicts does not prove harmful. The presence of an alcoholic in a place of work does not cause alcoholism in fellow workers, nor does the presence of a few drug addicts in a well balanced community threaten the health and safety of others. A young person who runs away from home and goes to live in a squat with a group of addicts is a different matter. In such circumstances there is substantial risk of drug abuse leading to addiction.

Kaleidoscope seeks to foster a good social life for the late night crowd in a downtown situation. The attention given to providing the right physical surroundings, the care given to the preparation and presentation of food, the skilful intervention of a large team of workers and a positive celebration of life are some of the ways by which Kaleidoscope attempts to give a better experience of life.

Kissing God is an extravagant way of speaking about using drugs. In the 1960s, many devotees of the drug cult believed that in moments of ecstasy they could achieve intimacy with God. It is doubtful if anyone familiar with the drug scene today would believe that.

It is perhaps coincidental that at the time when many theologians were turning their attention away from the supernatural elements in Christian belief, many people were seeking transcendental experience through meditation and through drugs. Christianity is nothing if it does not enable people to enter into union with God through a personal relationship with Christ. Kissing God is probably not a phrase a believer would use, but it is beautiful, similar in sentiment to Wesley's 'Jesus, lover of my soul'.

11: No Quick Fix

Today, the anti-drugs bandwagon is rolling at full speed. Politicians have become acutely and vocally concerned about the reported plans of international drugs organisations to market huge quantities of drugs in this country. Last year the number of registered drug addicts in Britain rose by 28 per cent to 10,200—and everyone working in the field agrees that this number represents only a small fraction of the real problem.

Many solutions have been proposed. There will be more police and customs officers allocated to the task of stopping drug trafficking and crash education programmes will aim to persuade young people against abusing drugs.

These efforts are useful, but do not go to the heart of the problem. Any strategy for preventing drug abuse needs to take account of all the factors which affect the wellbeing of children and young people. Housing, education and employment are all relevant in this context.

Equally important, I believe, is our spiritual environment. The drug culture of the 1950s and 1960s emerged at a time of spiritual decline in Britain. The hippy movement was a reaction against this—it was to a significant degree a spiritual movement. Hippies rejected the materialism of their parents and the capitalist philosophy of the politicians. They sought enlightenment and peace from eastern religions. To speed up the meditation associated with most religions, drugs were employed as a fast route to that state where the eye of the soul is opened and a person is at one with the universe.

Religious mystics strive hard to attain this blessedness through the contemplative life, with its long, slow growth and psychic storms. Hippies tried to gatecrash heaven with a quick fix of drugs.

Of course the hippy decade is now over. But young people in the 1980s have woken up to a bleak new day: unemployment, even greater accommodation problems for those unsupported by parents and a general sense of uncertainty.

For two millenia, Europe was inspired by the Ancient Greek ideals of truth, justice, beauty and public service. These ideals have been largely abandoned in favour of economic growth. Everything today is considered under economic headings. Harold Wilson advocated a quick fix of new technology to bring us to the promised land. Margaret Thatcher prescribed a quick fix of monetarism to bring Britain back to greatness. There is no quick fix.

The churches have a critical role in redressing this balance; in recovering the religious dimension of life. But churches can only animate society, like yeast in dough, to act as a preservative, like salt, if they re-engage in the life of their local communities. We cannot expect those looking for short-term practical relief from the problems of drug abuse to pursue, or even to understand this underlying need. Without an appreciation of the spiritual and social dimensions of the drug abuse problem, solutions are certain to prove shallow and short-lived.

Even at the most practical everyday level of policy-making on drug abuse, this distinction between the short-term, instant solution approach naturally favoured by politicians and the more careful, informed and sensitive route advocated by those with a deeper understanding is very marked.

For example, one of the most effective means for the

prevention of addiction is to identify children aged between 11 and 15 years, who are particularly vulnerable to drug abuse. We have had encouraging results working with children as young as 11 years, who have appeared on the drug scene, but who are not addicted. Some work along similar lines has been done in the USA.

At Kaleidoscope, we have identified a number of characteristics which enable us, with some degree of confidence, to recognise a potential drug abuser. Contrary to popular theory, the dominant characteristics are not broken or deprived homes. The relevant criteria we have observed are the following:

1. The child is in contact with drug abusers i.e. often out late at night mixing with an older group which includes drug users. The child may also have a mother or father dependent on alcohol or drugs.
2. The child shows signs of serious alienation from parents or school or from other stable peer groups.
3. The child has poor prospects of being successful in ways the parents had hoped e.g. a son or daughter of a professional family who fails 'A' levels and cannot see any way of achieving the standard of life to which he or she has been accustomed.
4. The child cannot identify with the religious or social expectations of the family e.g. parents of a girl in our hostel telephoned to say how glad they were that their daughter was going home at the weekend, but asked if we could suggest that she did not wear jeans, as this upset her grandmother.
5. The child has no ally easily accessible. A child, for a variety of complex reasons, may feel unsure of his or her relationship with either parent and be unable to turn to brothers, sisters or other close friends. Some adopted or illegitimate children feel insecure in this way.

Some individuals are able to cope in these situations, but a seriously insecure child may retreat into a private world or into the company of others who are experiencing a sense of alienation. This may involve a criminal gang, or a group which uses drugs. Drug abuse is particularly attractive because along with the occult, magic and certain kinds of music, it offers the possibility of private fulfilment.

Clearly whenever these criteria are discovered, urgent thought should be given to ways of providing comfort before the child seeks a potentially destructive solution. Where the situation demands it, a young person who has a strong wish to leave home will probably benefit from a place in a good hostel. Unfortunately, such hostels are hard to find and funding for such placements is becoming harder to obtain. At present, Government categorisations for funding hostels effectively exclude young drug abusers who have not reached the stage of addiction. This is rather like refusing treatment to cancer patients in the early stages of their disease.

Kaleidoscope's hostel has proved its value time and again to young drug abusers. By providing the positive environment of the hostel, where no more than four out of 20 residents at any one time will be drug abusers, intensive support can be provided. Through the club and day surgery, up to 40 others can be treated on a non-residential basis.

Kaleidoscope's approach is not the only correct one. Hospital drug dependency units, the backbone of the National Health Service's contribution and consumer of the lion's share of Government funding, continue to play a part. But these units see only a tiny proportion of addicts and have suffered a debilitating crisis of confidence over the issuing of maintenance prescriptions to drug users, since some of these drugs found their way quickly into the black market. In practice, most of the innovation in dealing with drug abuse has come from the voluntary sector.

Woman magazine, for example, in a recent article, contrasted the 'tough untender way' of Phoenix House with the 'softly, softly cure' of Kaleidoscope.

Phoenix House is a rehabilitation house—a gracious mansion standing in its own grounds where drug abusers are required to follow a strict regime of behaviour modification over a period of up to two years.

Different people do find help in different programmes. Many people have done well at Phoenix House, but many other addicts do not need such drastic treatment and, more to the point, less than one per cent of addicts will accept the programme voluntarily. Many, however, will accept rehabilitation houses as a court-ordered alternative to prison.

Kaleidoscope's 'softly, softly', or perhaps more accurately 'slowly, slowly' way involves trying to deal with an individual's need to blank out, rather than only with his or her drug-taking. Sometimes we are accused of not caring whether or not our people come off drugs.

But we know from experience that if a person becomes involved in other activities and finds new interests, this dependency upon drugs will decrease. We also know that if a person does not find a new way of life, simply withdrawing from drugs will only leave that individual vulnerable to further drug abuse, alcoholism or some other form of escape. Kaleidoscope's newly built art workshop and education unit, is designed for this very purpose. Showing people that life has a much wider range of desirable possibilities and putting them within reach is what Kaleidoscope is about.

This is also what the church is about, or at least what it should be about. Christ spoke of 'abundant life'. Christians believe that fullness of life can be found in God alone. That does not mean that religion must be offered as a kind of opiate. True faith in God must be experienced as enthusiastic living. Life is very, very good. Food and flowers, arts and crafts, books and films, music and languages, architecture and liturgy; all these, and everything else besides, is what is meant by God as creator. Humans are made in God's image—creative beings of endless potential.

Essential to this concept is freedom and variety. It is a denial of creativity to pursue conformity or to require individuals to follow a pre-determined pattern without their true consent. Many medically and religiously inspired projects for drug abusers have violated this fundamental truth. This violation occurs all too often because would-be care agencies are in search of an illusory quick fix for their clients' problems.

On many occasions I have had to suffer the rebuke of zealous Christians who have criticised the fact that we do not actively evangelise in the Kaleidoscope club. Private conversations cover all topics, including religious faith if someone raises the subject. But there are no posters declaring that God is good. We prefer to serve good coffee. There is no religious epilogue; we prefer to get on with the cleaning. This is not because we are cowards. It is because we believe that words about God have often been cheap.

The example of Christ is that he spoke in parables and gave signs of the kingdom, because he recognised that truth can only be received when the heart is prepared.

The present resurgence of social concern among Christians of all theological persuasions is most encouraging. Dr John Stott, a leading evangelical, said recently:

'Jesus himself sometimes did good works before proclaiming

the good news of the kingdom. Much missionary, medical, agricultural and nutritional work has opened the way to the gospel. If we turn a blind eye to people's suffering we must not be surprised if they turn a deaf ear to our message. Again, it isn't wrong to feed the hungry in a famine stricken area without it being an essential on every occasion to preach the gospel.'

Where churches are seriously considering involvement in the life of their local communities, they may wish to study the story of Kaleidoscope. It is not that there is a need for numerous church-based drug projects—the needs of a suburban community or industrial zone would be different. But the requirement to serve the needs of the local community by means of projects developed steadily over many years is the same everywhere. Love of God and love of our neighbours belong together. We must not give priority to one over the other.

The parables of the kingdom of God in the gospels are about slow and steady growth; about harvests and natural processes. Quick results, quick fixes are not implied.

12: Church Life

From the Kaleidoscope office, a door leads to a small prayer chapel. A shaft of light from a painted window throws a pattern of colours on to the stone floor. A sanctuary lamp glows by an icon. Candles provide living light around the chalice and paten and a spotlight focuses upon a bronze Celtic cross.

The small group which meets during the week to celebrate holy communion is part of that same tradition which led to breaking bread with Jan, David and Andrea in the early days of Kaleidoscope. The Eucharist has become the central focus of worship at the John Bunyan Baptist Church.

The form of the weekday communion begins with confession and follows with a psalm, intercession, the Gospel appointed for the day in the lectionary, reflection, the eucharistic prayer and the sharing of bread and wine. It ends, like the Sunday Eucharist, with the exhortation: 'Go, you are sent into the world to serve.'

It has become an essential and purposeful part of the community's life. Faced with constant, but unpredictable pressure and challenges beyond anyone's certain personal resources, the need for forgiveness, for nourishment and for intercession on behalf of the world. It is a reinforcing of the church's belief in the priestliness of its mission; a statement about the priesthood of all believers.

On Sundays, the church worships in the large chapel, constructed in the form of an irregular, eight-sided shape.

This allows the congregation to face a central communion table, which stands beneath the central cruciform shape of the concrete ceiling. The lighting is designed to emphasise further the central place of the Eucharist in the life of the congregation.

One of the beauties of Sunday worship is the variety of the worshippers. All lifestyles and age groups are represented and there is an approximately equal number of males and females. Some dress up for the occasion. Others wear informal or unconventional clothes. Some residents from the hostel and club attend, but most do not.

There is a regular liturgy, which has been prepared by the church membership and reflects the different Christian traditions they represent. The pattern is the traditional two-part practice found in the Roman Catholic and Anglican churches—the liturgy of the word and the liturgy of the breaking of bread. The liturgy, however, is shorter and simpler than is the case in the catholic tradition—making room for at least a 20 minute sermon in a one-hour service of worship.

The effect is that newcomers and strangers to John Bunyan church can recognise the dynamic of the liturgy. The form also lends itself to participation by members of the congregation in reading, singing and in the speaking parts of the liturgy. Baptists would recognise the style of hymn singing and the importance attached to preaching; they would also instantly understand the function of the open baptistry.

The church has become profoundly ecumenical as a consequence of its initial decision to serve the local community. It was inevitable that as part of that community a church with an open membership constitution would acquire members from many traditions.

Although loyalty to the Baptist denomination and its

principle of autonomous church government is cherished, several aspects of church life would seem strange to some Baptists.

The church's diaconate—an elected body which shares with the minister the responsibility of overseeing the church—has been opened to members of all denominations. One current deacon is a Roman Catholic.

This has meant the church coming to a common understanding of the meaning of eucharist. The word 'transsubstantiation' is avoided because it would need someone skilled in Aristotelian philosophy to be able to interpret it. Rather, an illustration is used. A lighthouse maybe purchased and used as a home. This change is decisive; it would no longer be regarded by Trinity House as a lighthouse, although its basic structure might remain unaltered. It is essentially a home. In the same way, the bread and wine consecrated within the context of the whole service is no longer used as bread and wine. It would indeed be desecration to take the bread and wine merely to satisfy individual hunger or thirst. The bread and wine retain the molecular structure of food and represent the world of nature and human endeavour. Offered in worship, the elements become for the believer, a sharing in the body and blood of Christ through the power of the Holy Spirit.

At Bunyan, the heart of the gospel is seen to be God's acceptance of sinful people. Jesus turned no one away. It is for this reason that in the church the good news of God's forgiveness is proclaimed to all and holy communion is offered to all. It is essential if salvation is to be fully realised that a person comes to mature understanding and firm faith, but that is more often a process than a blinding revelation. In any case, salvation depends upon God's grace primarily and only secondarily is it realised by personal faith.

It follows from this that children are included in the invitation to receive communion.

Likewise, saving grace is not confined to the church or even to Christians. On Friday night in the club, a wife of one of the Road Rats had her blouse partly open, revealing a crucifix. She did not express any religious faith, but when she described the difficulties facing a friend whose husband had just come out of prison, her sensitivity to her friend's needs was apparent. She was, in a sense, a priest to her friend. Many Christians do not recognise any such grace in a person who has not made an adequate profession of faith in Christ, but Jesus accepted the validity of faith, even of those with no stated religious convictions.

This openness in the life of the John Bunyan church does not mean that theology is accorded little importance. People who have had no previous church connections and others from different denominations are apt to ask the most penetrating questions. Theological discussion is part of the constant life of the church.

Special attention is given to the instruction of children, who participate fully in the normal worship of the church. From time to time, children go away together for a long weekend, which includes study of the faith.

Retreat weekends are also arranged for adults and bible study is encouraged through a regular study course based on the GCE A-level syllabus. This aspect of church life will take a major step forward when work is complete on a chapel in the grounds of our cottage in mid-Wales. Formerly a small barn, this building is being re-roofed, following a donation from the family of Sister Frances Makower, a Roman Catholic nun who has worked for several years on the Kaleidoscope staff.

The Pencilmaren chapel will be of great value to the people of Bunyan, most of whom live with the stresses of life in a big city and who need time and space to reflect and to grow. Other Pencilmaren buildings have been adapted to provide sleeping accommodation for visitors and the opportunity for discussion.

Most of the staff of Kaleidoscope are residential and this communal life encourages big celebrations. Friday night club is a highlight in many people's week, as is Sunday worship for many in the project. But there are other red-letter days in the calendar.

The pantomime, written and performed by church members and Kaleidoscope people, is an occasion of great fun. Christmas, too, is a very special occasion. Many residents go home for Christmas, but some have no home to go to. Some ex-residents return for Christmas.

Christmas celebrations begin on the Friday night before Christmas, when mince pies are given away at midnight in the club. The presence of many Catholics has promoted the high celebration of Christmas Eve. Christmas Eve Mass has not been copied, but many of the features have been examined and then incorporated in a fresh way.

When people arrive at the church on Christmas Eve, they are met by a child who hands them a white and gold stole. The stole is the mark of priesthood, indicating that every worshipper is acting as a priest to help offer up to God praise and thanksgiving on this holy night. The entire congregation facing the central communion table is thus robed in white and gold.

The eucharistic prayer traditionally begins with the exhortation, 'Lift up your hearts.' This phrase is commonly misunderstood as an appeal to everyone to try to create an exalted state of mind. Such an appeal would be difficult to obey. It is really a reminder to the congregation that they are in communion with heaven. (Hebrews 12: 22–24, Revelation 4.)

To help everyone realise this, incense is offered at the holy table, during the special Christmas prayer of thanksgiving (Revelation 8: 2–4). After holy communion, all gather round the table holding lighted tapers and singing 'Oh, come all ye faithful.'

All senses are involved in worship and from the moment of entry into the candlelit church, it is apparent to everyone that this is indeed a high celebration. The same is true of Christmas dinner served in the club next day. The tables are set and the room is richly decorated. Food in the club is normally vegetarian, but on Christmas Day, turkey, Christmas pudding and mince pies are served. Alcohol is not served in the club, but on Christmas Day hot brandy is poured over the puddings and set on fire. Afterwards there are presents and games.

Holy Week celebrations are just as exciting. On Maundy Thursday, a passover meal is served in the chapel. The lady in charge of the meal lights two candles, after which the Hebrew graces are said. I usually preside and the youngest child who can talk asks the four traditional passover questions: 'Why on this night do we eat unleavened bread?'; 'Why on this night do we eat bitter herbs?'; 'Why on this night do we dip the herbs twice?'; and 'Why on this night do we eat in a leisurely fashion?'

After supper, the ministers take towels and, accompanied by a deacon with a bowl of water, they wash the hands of everyone at the meal. Each individual is greeted and some appropriate remark is made.

'Edith, we honour you as being our oldest member . . . '

'Mary, you are to be received into membership tonight . . . '

'Mark, you are the youngest boy . . . '

'Alan, you are our faithful secretary,' and so on, round the tables.

Bread and wine served during the meal are then consecrated

for holy communion. All partake, including the children. The household of faith celebrates the Lord's supper.

On Good Friday, a form of the Stations of the Cross takes place. The fourteen traditional stages in Christ's journey to the cross are observed and different people lead a few minutes devotion at each stage. One person composes a prayer, another sings a verse, a third reads from a book or shares thoughts on a theme. Afterwards, eucharistic bread and wine are uncovered, but holy communion is not given on this day which commemorates the death of our Lord.

Easter Sunday is bright with flowers, candles and joyful singing. The Easter hymns repeat Alleluias over and over again. The ministers are robed in white. There are flowers and Easter eggs at lunch in the club afterwards.

The life of the church; the life of Kaleidoscope must encompass such celebration, just as it must embrace the world's bitterness and failure. The bread is broken and the wine outpoured in the Eucharist as both a commemoration of the death of Jesus and as a celebration of eternal life.

The state cannot nurture the life of a community—it is too big. It is practically impossible to bring together the youth department, the health department, the social services department, the education department and the housing department in a single enterprise. It needs people to take an overall view of the community and to accept responsibility.

Statutory services carry out statutory provisions. The church, seeking to love God and humanity, must carry out deeds of love. That is the nature of the church. The state can provide nurseries to help with the care of children, but it cannot replace human love.

God is love. The Kingdom of God is where love reigns. Kaleidoscope is not the Kingdom of God. But it strives to build that Kingdom in one small part of London.

Postscript

Not all newspaper headlines are bad. On March 14, 1985, the *Baptist Times* front page carried an item headed. 'POLICE BACK MINISTER IN DRUG BATTLE'.

The story reported the fact that Sir Kenneth Newman, head of the Metropolitan Police, had presented Kaleidoscope with a cheque for £5,000 towards the project's work with drug abusers.

Chief Inspector Ted Large, community liaison officer for Kingston, had recommended Kaleidoscope for the award. He told the *Baptist Times*, 'The Kaleidoscope project is somewhere I am confident to refer addicts. I know they will get professional help there. And it's somewhere the addicts feel there are people they can trust. We need more Kaleidoscopes.'

Although we greatly appreciate the generosity of this comment, we are not seeking to produce 'more Kaleidoscopes'. It is true that we receive a constant stream of visitors wanting to examine our model and that a handful of similar community-based projects now exist. But a multiplication of projects copying the Kaleidoscope philosophy would not be a good thing. All situations are different.

I do hope, however, that Kaleidoscope will prove an inspiration and in some way an exemplary model for new initiatives. In particular, it is my conviction that churches should accept the challenge of involvement in their local communities.

E.L.B.